Teacher's Handbook

ECCE ROMANI

A Latin Reading Program
Revised Edition

4
Pastimes and Ceremonies

Longman

Ecce Romani   Teacher's Handbook 4

ISBN 0 8013 0447 4
(78257)

Cover illustration by Judy Hans Price.

This edition of ECCE ROMANI is based on ECCE ROMANI A LATIN READING COURSE, originally prepared by The Scottish Classics Group © copyright The Scottish Classics Group 1971, 1982, and published in the United Kingdom by Oliver and Boyd, a Division of Longman Group. This revised edition has been prepared by a team of American and Canadian educators:
  Authors: Professor Gilbert Lawall, University of Massachusetts, Amherst, Massachusetts
  Consultants: Dr. Rudolph Masciantonio, Philadelphia Public Schools, Pennsylvania
        Ronald B. Palma, Holland Hall School, Tulsa, Oklahoma
        Dr. Edward Barnes, C. W. Jefferys Secondary School, Downsview, Ontario
        Shirley Lowe, Wayland Public Schools, Massachusetts

Acknowledgments:
Excerpts from *Confessions of St. Augustine*, translation and introduction by John K. Ryan. Copyright © 1960 by Doubleday & Company, Inc. Reprinted by permission of the publisher.

"Pyramus and Thisbe" extract from Ovid's *Metamorphoses*, translated by Rolfe Humphries © 1955 by Indiana University Press, © renewed 1983 by Winifred Davies. Reprinted by permission of Indiana University Press.

Bridal hymn from *Gaius Valerius Catullus: The Complete Poetry*, translated, with an introduction by Frank O. Copley. Copyright © 1957 by the University of Michigan. Reprinted by permission of the University of Michigan Press.

Vergil extract reprinted by permission of Macmillan Publishing Company from Vergil, *The Aeneid*, translated by Frank O. Copley. Copyright © 1965 by Macmillan Publishing Company.

Seneca letters reprinted by permission of the publishers and the Loeb Classical Library from *Seneca Ad Lucilium Epistulae Morales*, translated by Richard M. Gummere, Cambridge, Mass.: Harvard University Press, 1917.

Augustus extract reprinted by permission of the publishers and the Loeb Classical Library from *The Scriptores Historiae Augustae*, translated by David Magie, Cambridge, Mass.: Harvard University Press, 1917.

Pliny extract reprinted by permission of the publishers and the Loeb Classical Library from Pliny *Natural History*, translated by H. Rackham, Cambridge, Mass.: Harvard University Press, 1940.

Longman
95 Church Street
White Plains, New York 10601

Associated companies:
Longman Group Ltd., London
Longman Cheshire Pty., Melbourne
Longman Paul Pty., Auckland
Copp Clark Pitman, Toronto
Pitman Publishing Inc., New York

ABCDEFGHIJ-CT-959493929190

Contents

Introduction to Book 4: Pastimes and Ceremonies

At the beginning of this fourth teacher's handbook will be found a cumulative review of books 1 to 3 which may be used either after book 3 at the end of Latin I or before beginning book 4 in Latin II. This review section may be reproduced by teachers for use with their students.

We do not include a sample examination at the end of the fourth language activity book because teachers' goals, objectives, and testing strategies tend to diverge considerably by this time in the Latin program and we leave it up to individual teachers to devise their own testing instruments.

The final word study in the student's book treats the relationship of Latin to the Romance languages, and this relationship will be explored further in the word study sections of the fifth student's book and the fifth language activity book.

The major new grammar in the fourth book involves subordinate constructions using subjunctives, participles, and infinitives. The subjunctive constructions include **cum** circumstantial and causal clauses, indirect questions, result clauses, indirect commands, and purpose clauses. Constructions with participles include use of perfect passive participles and ablative absolutes. A sequence of four chapters deals with infinitives in indirect statements. The cultural content of the stories in the first half of the book moves from recreation (baths) and entertainment (recitations of poetry) to childrens' games and public entertainment in the arena (gladiatorial shows and wild-beast fights). In the second half of the book appear public ceremonies marking key phases in the life of typical Romans—coming of age, marriage, death, and funerals. While the main story line continues to focus on the Cornelius family, a number of figures from legend and history appear throughout the book, and their stories are woven into the main narrative: Pyramus and Thisbe, Androcles and the lion, Papirius Praetextatus, Arria, Catullus, and others. The final reading from a letter of Pliny in the language activity book incorporates a number of the themes of the second half of the book, in particular, marriage, death, and funerals. Authentic Roman voices are thus allowed to speak for themselves amid the main theme of the fictional Cornelius family.

Teachers should consult the Bibliography at the end of this handbook for a list of basic, highly recommended background and source books for the cultural topics. The cultural background readings grouped as the next to the last section of this handbook provide further original source material in English on the baths, Pyramus and Thisbe, wild-beast hunts, opposition to the games, weddings, and Roman funerals.

There are 418 new words in the student's book; they are marked in the vocabulary at the end of the book with numbers indicating the chapter in which they first appear. English-Latin vocabularies for all of the English to Latin translation exercises in the chapters and review sections of the language activity book are provided at the back of this teacher's handbook. Also provided there are other word lists, one set of which includes designation of words that occur in Colby's *Latin Word Lists* for first and second years and one of which lists the verbs of which the principal parts are to be mastered as students progress through the chapters of the fourth student's book.

As in the third teacher's handbook, we provide suggestions for written work in English based on the cultural content of the stories and the background readings in English and in Latin. We urge teachers to incorporate a continuing program of writing in English into the Latin course and to stress transfer of skills developed in the learning of Latin to the development and perfecting of structure and style in the student's written English.

Beginning in the second student's book, we have been introducing the students to real Latin in the form of **sententiae** from ancient authors, graffiti, and brief extracts from Latin literature—all at appropriate points in the chapters of the student's book. The fourth student's book and accompanying language activity book introduce considerably more real Latin and prepare for the transition to regular readings in real Latin in the fifth book. Apart from the **sententiae**, extracts from the following authors or sources are included (usually with accompanying English translations) in the fourth student's book: Plautus (Chapter 42; 3 lines), Horace (Chapter 43; 3 lines), graffiti (Chapter 43; 8 lines), Ovid (Chapter 44; 14 lines), graffiti (Chapter 46; 12 lines), Seneca (Chapter 48; 10 lines), Gellius (Chapter 49; 9 lines), Cicero (Chapter 50; 6 lines), Martial (Chapter 52; 4 lines), epitaphs (Chapter 53; 16 lines), and Catullus (Chapter 53; 10 lines). There are a total of 95 lines of real Latin here. The **Versiculī** contain 37 lines of Martial and 20 of Catullus. In the language activity book there are 116 lines of real Latin (24 of Ovid's Pyramus and Thisbe, 23 of Gellius' Androcles and the Lion, 7 of Cicero on the games, 21 of Gellius on Papirius Praetextatus, 10 of Pliny on Arria, and 31 of Pliny on the death of the daughter of Fundanus). Four of the passages are the original Latin versions of stories that are previewed in adapted versions in the student's book. Initially the difference between the adapted version in the student's book (e.g., the story of Pyramus and Thisbe in Chapter 43) and the original in the language activity book is considerable. Only segments of the original story are given for students to translate in the language activity book, and they are accompanied by appropriate glosses. The student's familiarity with the story, its sentence structures, and its vocabulary from their reading in the student's book will greatly ease the task of translating the original version in the language activity book. Segments of Gellius' original version of the story of Androcles and the lion are given in the language activity book exercises for the chapter (47) that introduces this story in the student's book, and the entire stories of Papirius Praetextatus and of Arria from Gellius and Pliny, respectively, are given in the language activity book after these stories are read in only slightly adapted versions in the student's book (Chapters 51 and 52).

There is a deliberate progression here. The stories in the student's book undergo less and less adaptation from the original, and more and more of the original story is given in the language activity book. The culmination of both of these developments comes in the final chapter of the language activity book where an entire letter of Pliny is given in unadapted form with no preview of it in the student's book. Teachers having their students study all of the original Latin in the chapters of the fourth student's book, the **Versiculī**, and the fourth language activity book will have covered a total of 268 lines of real Latin in the course of their use of these books. This exposure to the complexities of real Latin will provide an excellent foundation for the reading of unadapted passages in the fifth student's book and its accompanying language activity book.

Cumulative Review of Books 1–3

The following Cumulative Review of Books 1–3 provides a structured review of the main grammatical features introduced in the entire course up to this point. It may be duplicated for use by students. We recommend that several days of class time be spent on this review and that parts of it be assigned for written work. The teacher may wish to consult the sections titled Syntax at the ends of the first three teacher's handbooks as preparation and support for this cumulative review. The grammatical features reviewed here include the following:

a. all cases of nouns of all five declensions
b. adjectives of the 1st and 2nd declensions and of the 3rd declension, positive, comparative, and superlative, and agreement of adjectives with nouns
c. the personal pronouns (**ego**, **tū**, etc.), in all forms except the genitive; the relative pronoun; the demonstrative pronouns and adjectives (**hic**, **ille**, and **is**)
d. adverbs (positive, comparative, and superlative)
e. numbers
f. prepositional phrases
g. place and time clues and expressions
h. subordinate clauses introduced with many different conjunctions
i. all forms of regular and irregular verbs in the indicative mood, active and passive
j. deponent verbs
k. present infinitives (active and passive)
l. perfect infinitives (active)
m. participles (perfect passive and present active)
n. imperatives (positive and negative, active and passive)

Not included are the imperfect and pluperfect subjunctive forms. We do include a brief exercise on perfect active infinitives.

There are four parts to the Cumulative Review, each based on a reading passage. The grammatical material reviewed in each part is organized as follows (numbers in parentheses indicate chapters that may be consulted for review):

Part 1: Prepositional Phrases (9)
        Irregular Verbs (8, 17, 22)
        Place Clues (37)
        Time Clues (37)

Part 2: Nouns (21)
    Adjectives (17, 32)
    Present Infinitives (6, 29)

Part 3: Numbers (15, 36)
    Pronouns and Demonstrative Adjectives (21, 25, 27, 29)
    Adverbs (33)
    Active and Passive Verbs (10, 14, 17, 19, 22, 23, 25, 28, 30)
    Imperatives (10, 17, 35)

Part 4: Participles (31, 38)
    Perfect Active Infinitive (40)
    Deponent Verbs (35)
    Subordinate Clauses (passim)

In Activity CR1c, No. 4, **sub** is to be deduced in the sense "at the foot of"; in No. 7, **pūrissima** is to be deduced. In Activity CR2a, **iocōsus** (30) is to be deduced. In Activity CR4a, **Puellīs . . . reductīs. . . .** (33) is not an ablative absolute but a dative with **inquit**; the gerund in the phrase **fīnem fābulās nārrandī** (42) is not likely to cause students trouble, but if it does it may be simply translated by the teacher.

The following are sample translations of the English sentences in Activity CR4e, No. 5:
    a. Dum puellae trāns Tiberim natābant, custōdēs hastās in eās iaciēbant.
    b. Dum Rōmānī fortitūdinem puellārum laudant, in Viā Sacrā statuam Cloeliae posuērunt.

PART 1: PLANNING A JOURNEY

Activity CR1a

Read aloud and translate:

Cornēlius cum familiā iam diū Rōmae erat. Hodiē, a.d. IV Nōnās Augustās, Cornēlius multās hōrās in Forō occupātus erat. Vesperī Marcus et Sextus in ātriō lūdēbant cum intrāvit Cornēlius.

"Crās," inquit, "amīcum vīsitāre dēbeō. Haud 5 longē ab urbe Rōmā Tusculī habitat. Quattuor post diēbus Rōmam regrediar. Vīsne mēcum venīre, Marce? Sextus quoque nōbīscum veniet, sī nōn molestus erit."

Rogāvit Marcus, "In raedā iter faciēmus, pater?" 10

Cui respondit pater, "Minimē vērō! Māter tua nōbīscum venīre nōn vult. Itaque in raedā iter nōn faciēmus. Servōs iubēbō equōs parāre. Equīs nōs Tusculum portābimur. Ita ad vīllam amīcī celeriter adveniēmus." 15

Eō tempore tamen Cornēlia in ātrium intrāvit. "Quid audiō?" inquit. "Ad vīllam amīcī iter facere in animō habēs, pater? Cūr nōn mē eō tēcum dūcēs?"

At Sextus, "Puellae semper sunt molestae. Cūr 20 nōn domī cum mātre manēs, Cornēlia? Semper tū nōbīscum venīre vīs."

Cornēlius tamen, "Tacē, Sexte!" inquit. "Sī Cornēlia nōbīscum venīre vult, licet. Servōs iubēbō rae-

dam extrā portam Flāminiam parāre. Crās māne 25 abībimus. Ante noctem ad vīllam pervenīre in animō habeō. In caupōnam iterum dēvertere nōlō."

haud, not
dēvertō, dēvertere (3), **dēvertī, dēversum**, to turn aside, spend the night

Activity CR1b

Prepositional Phrases

Locate 20 prepositional phrases in the reading passage above.

Activity CR1c

Prepositional Phrases

Select, read aloud, and translate:

1. Per (tōtō diē/tōtum diem) Cornēlius in (Forō/Forum) occupātus erat.
2. Ad (vīllam/vīllā) per (Viae Appiae/Viam Appiam) crās ībimus.
3. Interdiū intrā (urbem/urbe) raedās agere nōn licet.
4. Vīlla amīcī Cornēliī est prope (Tusculō/Tusculum) sub (montem pulchrum/monte pulchrō).
5. Ad (iānuā/iānuam) vīllae iānitor dormiet.
6. "Nārrā mihi dē (vīllā/vīllam) amīcī tuī," inquit Cornēlia.
7. "Vīlla sita est inter (duōs montēs/duōbus montibus)," inquit Cornēlius, "et nōn est sine (aquam pūrissimam/aquā pūrissimā)."
8. Quam diū apud (amīcō tuō/amīcum tuum) manēbimus?" rogat Cornēlia.
9. Paucīs diēbus ē (vīllā/vīllam) ēgrediēmur et Rōmam reveniēmus.

Activity CR1d

Irregular Verbs

1. *Locate three occurrences of forms of the verb **volō** in the reading passage in Activity CR1a above.*
2. *Locate two occurrences of forms of the verb **nōlō** in the reading passage in Activity CR1a above.*

Activity CR1e

Irregular Verbs

Change the main verb in each of the following sentences from singular to plural or from plural to singular, keeping the same person, number and tense. Make other changes in the sentence as necessary. Read the new sentence aloud and translate it.

1. Nōlō hodiē ad vīllam īre.
2. Crās puella ad vīllam īre nōlet.
3. Heri ad vīllam īre nōlēbātis.
4. Heri ad vīllam ībāmus.
5. Ad vīllam hodiē nōn potes īre.
6. Puella ad vīllam hodiē nōn it.
7. Nōlīte īre hodiē!

8. Crās ad vīllam ī!
9. Estisne dēfessī?
10. Servī, ferte cistās ad raedam!
11. Cistās ad raedam fers.
12. Servī cistās ad raedam ferunt.
13. Equī poterunt nōs ad vīllam ferre.
14. Crās poterō ad vīllam īre.
15. Crās erō Tusculī.
16. Herī erās Rōmae.
17. Crās ad vīllam īre volēs.
18. Crās ad vīllam nōn ībō.
19. Hodiē ad vīllam īre volō.
20. Heri ad vīllam īre poterat.
21. Crās ad vīllam īre vultis.

Activity CR1f

Place Clues

Using the reading passage in Activity CR1a above as a guide, give the Latin for:

1. in (*or* at) Rome
2. in the Forum
3. from the city (of) Rome
4. in Tusculum
5. to Rome
6. to Tusculum
7. to the country house
8. into the atrium
9. at home
10. in the atrium

Activity CR1g

Place Clues

Give the Latin for the phrases in italics in the following sentences:

1. They were going *to Brundisium.*
2. They stayed *at Brundisium.*
3. After three days he went away *from Brundisium.*
4. We will return *home* in the summer.
5. Flavia lives *in a neighboring farmhouse.*
6. Tomorrow we will depart *from Rome.*
7. After three days we will return *to Rome.*
8. We spend the whole summer *at Baiae.*
9. Next summer we will return *to Baiae.*
10. Cornelius and his family were *at home in Rome* for a long time.

Activity CR1h

Time Clues

Using the reading passage in Activity CR1a above as a guide, give the Latin for:

1. for a long time now
2. for many hours
3. in the evening
4. after four days

5. at that moment (time)
6. before night(fall)

Activity CR1i

Time Clues

Give the Latin for the italicized phrases in the following sentences:

1. *Three days later* we will return to Rome.
2. Cornelius was occupied in the Forum *for five hours.*
3. *Before the third hour* Cornelius was already tired.
4. *In three hours* he will depart for Tusculum.
5. Cornelius arrived at the Forum *three hours ago.*
6. *At that very moment (time)* he was not tired.

PART 2: HEADING FOR TUSCULUM

Activity CR2a

Read aloud and translate:

Postrīdiē raeda ā servīs parāta est extrā Portam Caelimontānam. Ibi servī cum raedā Cornēlium līberōsque exspectābant.

Prīmā lūce Cornēlius lectīcās condūxit et cūnctī celeriter portam petīvērunt. Dum per viās Rōmae 5 tumultūs plēnās ībant, līberī turbās cīvium adstantium et hūc illūc concursantium spectābant. Templa ingentia et aedificia ēlegantissima urbis admīrābantur. Mox ad Portam Caelimontānam pervēnērunt. In raedam ascendērunt. Iam per Viam Tusculānam 10 in itinere profectī sunt. Puerī servōs in agrīs et vīneīs labōrantēs vidēbant. Viātōrēs in viā ambulantēs quoque spectābant. Cornēlia tamen dormiēbat quod diēs iam erat calidior.

Subitō raedārius puerīs clāmāvit, "Puerī, spectāte! Ecce, mīlitēs!" Puerī laetī Cornēliam excitāvē- 15 runt. Cornēlia īrācunda mīlitēs spectāvit quī iter per viam celeriter faciēbant. Nunc dormīre nōn poterat.

Itaque, "Sī iter est longum, pater," inquit, "cūr nōn fābulam nōbīs nārrās? Fābulam dē puellā nōbīs 20 nārrā! Illās fābulās nōn amō quae dē virīs fortibus nārrantur. Nōnne fābulam dē puellā praeclārissimā celeberrimāque nārrāre potes?"

"Nūllae sunt puellae praeclārissimae," Cornēliae Sextus inquit. 25

Sed Marcus, "Eucleidēs mihi fābulam dē Atalantā nūper nārrāvit—"

Sextus procācī cum rīsū interpellāvit, "Dē puellā quae nōmen tam rīdiculum habēbat audīre nōlō. Dē rēbus iocōsīs audīre volō." 30

Marcus tamen, "Sī soror mea dē Atalantā audīre vult, mihi placet. Dē Atalantā, pater, nōbīs nārrā!"

Activity CR2b

Nouns

Match each noun at the left (taken from the designated line in the reading passage in Activity CR2a above) first with its case and then with its use within the phrase or sentence in which it occurs:

1. lūce (4)	A. vocative	a. direct object
2. tumultūs (6)	B. nominative	b. indirect object
3. urbis (8)	C. genitive	c. object of
4. raedam (10)	D. dative	preposition
5. viātōrēs (12)	E. accusative	d. subject
6. diēs (14)	F. ablative	e. direct address
7. puerīs (15)		f. possession
8. iter (17)		g. time
9. pater (19)		h. with adjective
10. rīsū (28)		
11. nōmen (29)		

Activity CR2c

Nouns

1. In the reading passage in Activity CR2a above, locate one noun of each declension (1st, 2nd, 3rd, 4th, and 5th).
2. Identify the gender, case, and number of each noun you locate as it appears in the passage.
3. Give the forms of each noun you locate in all of its cases, singular and plural.

Activity CR2d

Adjectives

The following adjectives are taken from the designated lines of the reading passage in Activity CR2a above.
1. For each adjective give the corresponding positive or comparative or superlative forms. Be sure your new forms agree with the noun that the adjective modifies.
2. Then give the best translation of the sentence first with the positive, then with the comparative, and finally with the superlative form of the adjective. Remember that the comparatives and superlatives can have different meanings, e.g., "more . . .," "rather . . .," "too . . ."; and "most . . .," "very . . .," "exceedingly . . ."

Positive	Comparative	Superlative
1. ingentia (8)	_____	_____
2. _____	calidior (14)	_____
3. īrācunda (17)	_____	_____
4. fortibus (21)	_____	_____
5. _____	_____	praeclārissimā celeberrimāque (22–23)
6. _____	_____	praeclārissimae (24)
7. procācī (28)	_____	_____
8. rīdiculum (29)	_____	_____
9. iocōsīs (30)	_____	_____

Activity CR2e

Adjectives

1. Give the comparative and superlative of each of the following adjectives.

2. Give an English word derived from each comparative and superlative form.
3. Give the meaning of each English derivative.

bonus   malus
magnus   parvus

Activity CR2f

Present infinitives

Locate in the reading passages in Activities CR1a and CR2a one example of a present infinitive used with each of the following verbs or phrases. Translate the sentence in which each occurs.

1. dēbeō
2. volō
3. nōlō
4. iubeō
5. in animō habeō
6. possum

Activity CR2g

Present Infinitives

The sentence **Servōs iubēbō equōs parāre** (Activity CR1a, line 13) may be rewritten with a passive infinitive as follows: **Ā servīs iubēbō equōs parārī**. Supply passive forms of the infinitives in parentheses to complete the following sentences. Translate each sentence.

1. Ā puerīs parvīs magnum aedificium _____ potest. (incendere)
2. Puerī temerāriī ā parentibus _____ vix possunt. (monēre)
3. Amīcus ā Cornēliō _____ dēbet. (vīsitāre)
4. Cornēlius ab amīcō Tusculī _____ dēbet. (excipere)
5. Fābula ā Cornēliā _____ nōn poterat, quod dormiēbat. (audīre)

PART 3: ATALANTA

Activity CR3a

Read aloud and translate:

Pater hanc fābulam nārrāre coepit.

Ōlim in Graeciā habitābat puella quaedam pulcherrima, nōmine Atalanta. Multī virī eam uxōrem dūcere volēbant. Atalanta tamen, quod celerrimē currere poterat, omnibus virīs, "Sī tū celerius quam 5
ego cucurreris," inquit, "ego uxor tua erō. Sī tamen ā mē victus eris, tū statim necāberis."

Dūrae certē erant eae condiciōnēs, sed multī currere volēbant. Ūnus, deinde alius fortūnam temptābat. Ēheu! Quamquam multī singulī cucurrērunt, 10
omnēs victī sunt; poenās dedērunt omnēs.

Inter spectātōrēs autem ōlim erat adulēscēns quīdam, nōmine Hippomenēs, quī, cum prīmum Atalantam vīdit, statim amāvit. Itaque, quamquam perī-

culōsissimum erat, currere cōnstituit. Amīcī eum 15
retinēre nōn poterant. Eīs, "Ego," inquit, "Atalantam vincere possum. Venus, quae amantibus favet,
mihi auxilium dabit." Deam igitur auxilium rogāvit;
illa eī tria māla aurea dedit et, "Hīs bene ūtere,"
inquit. 20

Diē cōnstitūtā et adulēscēns et puella summā ce-
leritāte currēbant. Hippomenēs, quod Atalanta prīmum locum iam sūmpserat, prīmum deinde secun-
dum ē tribus mālīs ante puellam currentem iēcit.
"Haec quidem māla," sēcum cōgitābat, "puellam ā 25
cursū āvertent."

Illa bis mālum petīvit. Ille bis puellam praeteriit.
Sed Atalanta, ubi clāmōrēs spectātōrum audīvit,
multō celerius cucurrit. Hippomenem praeteriit
atque fīnī cursūs iam appropinquābat. At Hippo- 30
menēs, "Nunc, ō dea," inquit, "fer mihi auxilium!"
Tum tertium mālum longē iēcit. Dum puella hoc
malum petit, Hippomenēs ad fīnem cursūs per-
vēnit. Victa est puella. Victor laetus ab arēnā
puellam dūxit. 35

> **dūrus, -a, -um**, harsh
> **diē cōnstitūtā**, on the appointed day
> **cursus, -ūs** (m), course, track
> **bis**, twice
> **ūtor, ūtī** (3), **ūsus sum** (+ *abl.*), to use
> **āvertō, āvertere** (3), **āvertī, āversum**, to turn away

Activity CR3b

Numbers

1. *Answer the following questions in Latin:*

   Quot māla Venus virō dedit?
   Quotum mālum Hippomenēs longē iēcit?

2. *Recite the cardinal numbers in Latin from one to twelve.*
3. *Give an English word derived from each of the Latin cardinal numbers from one to ten.*
4. *Recite the following ordinal numbers in numerical sequence:*

sextus	nōnus
quārtus	prīmus
duodecimus	septimus
secundus	mīllēsimus
centēsimus	vīcēsimus
octāvus	decimus
ūndecimus	quīntus
quīnquāgēsimus	quīngentēsimus
tertius	

Activity CR3c

Pronouns and Demonstrative Adjectives

1. *In the reading passage in Activity CR3a above, locate in sequence pronouns that mean:*

her	him	these
you	to them	she
I	to me	he
me	to him	

2. *In each of lines 1, 8, 25, and 32–33 of the reading passage in Activity CR3a above, locate a demonstrative adjective and the noun that it modifies. Give the gender, čase, and number of each adjective-noun combination.*
3. *Recite from memory all of the forms of the following pronouns and demonstrative adjectives:* **is, hic, ille.**
4. *In lines 12–20 of the reading passage in Activity CR3a above, locate two relative pronouns. Identify the antecedent of each relative pronoun. Then explain the gender, case, and number of each relative pronoun.*
5. *Fill in the correct forms of the relative pronoun in the following sentences:*

   a. Virī, _____ Atalanta vīcit, necātī sunt. (whom)
   b. Condiciōnēs, _____ Atalanta imposuit, dūrae erant. (which)
   c. Multī, _____ cucurrērunt, victī sunt. (who)
   d. Vir, _____ amīcī retinēre nōn poterant, erat Hippomenēs nōmine. (whom)
   e. Hippomenēs, _____ Venus māla dedit, Atalantam vincere potest. (to whom)
   f. Māla, _____ Venus virō dedit, erant aurea. (which)
   g. Spectātōrum clāmōrēs, _____ Atalanta incitāta est, erant magnī. (by which)
   h. Mālum, _____ Hippomenēs longissimē iēcit, erat tertium. (which)
   i. Atalanta, _____ Hippomenēs uxōrem dūxit, erat laeta. (whom)

Activity CR3d

Adverbs

1. *In lines 27–35 of the reading passage in Activity CR3a above, locate a positive adverb ending in* **-ē.** *In lines 2–7, locate a comparative and a superlative adverb.*
2. *Give the positive, comparative, and superlative adverbs made from each of the following adjectives:*

fēlīx	dīligēns
malus	bonus
longus	trīstis
magnus	multus

Activity CR3e

Active and Passive Verbs

1. *In lines 2–7 of the reading passage in Activity CR3a above, locate two passive verbs and identify their tenses. In lines 8–11, locate one passive verb and identify its tense. In lines 27–35, locate one passive verb and identify its tense.*
2. *Identify and explain the gender of any perfect passive participles used in the verb forms located in 1 above.*
3. *Give the requested forms of the following verbs first in the active voice and then in the passive voice in all of the tenses (present, imperfect, future, perfect, pluperfect, and future perfect). Give all of the active forms for each*

verb first and then all of the passive forms. Translate each form as you give it.

necō (2nd person pl.)
retineō (1st person pl.)
dūcō (2nd person sing.)
iaciō (3rd person pl.)
audiō (3rd person sing.)

Activity CR3f

Imperatives

1. *In the reading passage in Activity CR3a above, locate one imperative in lines 12–20 and one in lines 27–35.*
2. *Give the positive and negative imperatives, singular and plural, for each verb listed in Activity CR3e above, No. 3.*
3. *Give the positive and negative imperatives, singular and plural, for each of the following irregular verbs:*

esse
īre
ferre

PART 4: CLOELIA

Activity CR4a

Read aloud and translate:

Līberī patrem fābulam dē Atalantā nārrantem tacitī audīvērunt. Cum is fīnem fēcisset, "Pater," inquit Cornēlia, "nōnne puella Rōmāna quaedam sē fortissimam praebuit?"

"Ita vērō, mea parvula!" respondit Cornēlius. 5
"Nōmen illīus puellae erat Cloelia. Cloelia et amīcae eius obsidēs ad castra Porsennae, rēgis Etruriae, quī Rōmam obsidēbat, missae sunt. Eā nocte puellae erant trīstissimae. Lacrimantēs in castrīs sedēbant.

" 'Quōmodo umquam ex hīs castrīs incolumēs 10 ēvādēmus?' inquiunt. 'Quōmodo Rōmam regrediēmur? Neque patrēs neque mātrēs umquam posthāc vidēbimus?' Tandem, postquam multa tālia inter sē dīxērunt, obdormīvērunt.

"Māne tamen Cloelia, quae ad mediam noctem 15 vigilāverat, cōnsilium audāx cēterīs puellīs explicāvit.

" 'Hodiē,' inquit, 'cum advesperāverit, ē castrīs clam exīre cōnābimur. Necesse erit custōdēs dīligenter vītāre. Tum trāns Tiberim natābimus. Nōn 20 difficile erit ita Rōmam pervenīre. Ego nihil vereor; vōs quoque nōlīte verērī.'

"Vesperī igitur tacitae ē castrīs ēgressae in aquam dēsiluērunt. Subitō tamen custōdēs, quī sonitum aquae audīverant, eās cōnspexērunt. Ad rīpam flū- 25 minis celeriter dēcucurrērunt. Multās hastās in eās iaciēbant. Puellae tamen celeriter natantēs ad alteram rīpam Tiberis incolumēs advēnērunt.

"Porsenna, ubi audīvit puellās effūgisse, īrā commōtus nūntiōs statim Rōmam mīsit. 30

" 'Nisi hās obsidēs remīseritis,' inquiunt, 'urbem

incendēmus,' Itaque Rōmānī invītī puellās remīsērunt. Puellīs in castra reductīs Lars Porsenna, 'Obsidibus,' inquit, 'nōn licet ē castrīs ēgredī. Itaque vōs reprehendō quod ē castrīs aufūgistis. Sed vōs 35 laudō quod rem tam perīculōsam fēcistis, quamquam puellae modo estis. Itaque vōs Rōmam ad parentēs remittō.'

"Tum Rōmānī nōn modo fortitūdinem puellārum laudābant sed in Viā Sacrā statuam puellae equō 40 īnsidentis posuērunt."

Ita Cornēlius fīnem fābulās nārrandī fēcit et mox Tusculum advēnērunt.

praebeō (2), to show
obses, obsidis (m/f), hostage
posthāc, after this, again
īnsideō, īnsidēre (2), **īnsēdī, īnsessum** (+ dat.), to sit on

rīpa, -ae (f), bank
flūmen, flūminis (n), river
hasta, -ae (f), spear

Activity CR4b

Participles

1. a. *In the reading passage above, locate four present active participles (lines 1–4, 5–9, 23–28, and 39–41).*
   b. *Identify the gender, case, and number of each participle.*
   c. *Locate the noun which each participle modifies.*
2. *In the reading passage above, locate and then identify the gender, case, and number of the following:*
   a. *a perfect passive participle used as part of a perfect passive verb form (lines 5–9)*
   b. *a perfect participle of a deponent verb (lines 23–28)*
   c. *a perfect passive participle that is not used as part of a perfect passive verb form (lines 31–38)*
3. *For the participle located in 2c above, locate the noun which it modifies. Translate the sentence in which the participle occurs.*
4. *Translate the sentence in which you located a perfect participle of a deponent verb (2b above). Are the perfect participles of deponent verbs active or passive in form? in meaning?*
5. *Look at the sentences in which the four present active participles that you identified in 1 above occur. Translate each sentence carefully, showing that the action described by the present participle was taking place at the same time as the action of the main verb.*
6. *Look at the sentences in which the two perfect participles that you identified in 2b and c above occur. Translate each sentence carefully, showing that the action described by the perfect participle took place prior to the action of the main verb.*

Activity CR4c

Perfect Active Infinitive

1. *Locate one perfect active infinitive in lines 29–30 of the reading passage in Activity CR4a above and translate the sentence in which it occurs.*

2. *Give the perfect active infinitives of the following verbs:*

accipiō	afferō	conticēscō
dormiō	percutiō	nārrō
scindō	obsideō	cupiō
poscō	possum	resistō
parō	condō	veniō
volō		

Activity CR4d

Deponent Verbs

1. *In the reading passage in Activity CR4a above, locate three deponent verbs in the 1st person singular or plural (lines 10–14 and 18–22) and translate the sentences in which they occur.*

2. *In the reading passage in Activity CR4a above, locate two infinitives of deponent verbs (lines 18–22 and 31–38) and translate the sentences in which they occur.*

3. *Think of active verbs which are approximate synonyms of the deponent verbs located in 1 and 2 above, and substitute the corresponding forms (same tense, person, and number) of these verbs for the deponent verbs in the sentences.*

4. *Give the requested forms of the following deponent verbs in all of the tenses (present, imperfect, future, perfect, pluperfect, and future perfect). Translate each form as you give it.*

   moror (2nd person pl.)
   vereor (1st person pl.)
   loquor (2nd person sing.)
   regredior (3rd person pl.)
   experior (3rd person sing.)

5. *Give the positive and negative imperatives, singular and plural, for each verb listed in 4 above.*

Activity CR4e

Subordinate Clauses

1. *In the reading passage in Activity CR4a above, locate subordinate clauses that are introduced by the following subordinating conjunctions and relative pronouns, which are listed in the sequence in which they appear in the passage. Read aloud and translate each subordinate clause.*

cum	ubi
quī	nisi
postquam	quod
quae	quod
cum	quamquam
quī	

2. *Give English meanings for the following subordinating conjunctions that you have met but that do not appear in the reading passage in Activity CR4a above:*

dum	sī
nam	

3. *Answer the following questions:*
   a. *What does the conjunction **ubi** mean as used in line 29 of the reading passage in Activity CR4a above?*
   b. *What other meaning can this conjunction have?*
   c. *What does the conjunction **cum** mean as used in lines 2 and 18 of the reading passage in Activity CR4a above?*
   d. *What other meaning can this conjunction have?*
   e. *Translate the following sentences:*

   Dum raeda per viam ībat, puerī rūsticōs et agrōs spectābant. Dum puerī aedificia in Forō īnspiciunt, Cornēlium ē Cūriā ēgredientem cōnspexērunt.

4. *Answer the following questions, using the sentences above and your translations of them as guides:*
   a. *When **dum** appears in a subordinate clause with a verb in the imperfect tense, what does it mean?*
   b. *What does **dum** mean when it appears in a subordinate clause with a verb in the present tense in a sentence in which the main verb is in the perfect tense?*

5. *Using the reading passage in Activity CR4a above as a guide, give the Latin for:*
   a. As long as the girls were swimming across the Tiber, the guards were throwing spears at them.
   b. While the Romans were praising the bravery of the girls, they set up a statue of Cloelia in the Via Sacra.

Teaching Notes

CHAPTER 41: AT THE BATHS

Student's Book

1. Some distinction might be made between **balneae** and **thermae**. Baths built and kept up by private individuals as profit-making concerns were called **balneae,** and in imperial times there were large numbers of them both in Rome and throughout the empire. Bathrooms, where these existed in private homes, were also called **balneae**. The **thermae** were much larger, far more magnificent but few in number. They were built for public use by wealthy private individuals and later by the emperors, e.g., the Baths of Agrippa, Nero, Caracalla, and Diocletian. These were run for the state by contractors for a fixed sum of money, and the contractors charged a small entrance fee. There is more background material on the baths on pages 13–16 of the student's book.

Not much is known about the two games referred to; both were Greek in origin. In the game called **trigōn** (transliteration of a Greek word meaning "three-cornered"), there were three players who stood in a triangle. The three players had to agree about the method of throwing. The really expert players threw the ball and caught it using the left hand only.

Harpastum (transliteration of a Greek noun derived from a verb meaning "to snatch," "to seize") was undoubtedly a more strenuous game in which a ball, sometimes more than one ball, was thrown among the players. Each player tried to catch the ball thrown towards him.

2. **a.** Three uses of the subjunctive in subordinate clauses (all introduced in the third student's book) are discussed (indirect questions, **cum** circumstantial, and **cum** causal), and the forms of the imperfect and pluperfect subjunctive are tabulated.
   b. The stories begin with one of the most important pastimes of the Romans, the daily visit to the baths, which could include athletic and social as well as hygienic functions. Titus' visit to the baths concludes with a story of a bald-headed old man adapted from Petronius' *Satyricon* (27)—none other than the Trimalchio, with whom students will be familiar from the third student's book and the cultural background readings at the end of the third teacher's handbook.

3. Words to be deduced: **convenīre** (3), **varius** (8), **vapor** (13), **senātus** (19), and **rīdiculus** (21).

4. Structures:
   a. Anaphora:
   Aliī . . . , aliī . . . , aliī . . . , aliī. . . . (9)
   b. Condensed sentence:
   . . . cupiēbant cognōscere quid . . . agerētur, cūr . . . arcessīvisset, quae . . . admitterent. (18–20)

5. Uses of the subjunctive in the reading passage:
   a. Indirect Questions:
   . . . quid . . . agerētur, cūr . . . arcessīvisset, quae scelera . . . admitterent. (18–20)
   b. **Cum** Causal:
   . . . cum calōrem . . . vix patī possent, ... (12–13)
   . . . cum ille . . . vidērētur. . . . (17)
   c. **Cum** Circumstantial:
   . . . cum Titus pervēnisset, ... (4)
   Cum . . . sē . . . exercuissent, ... (10–11)
   Cum . . . regressī essent, ... (13–14)
   . . . cum manūs lāvisset, ... (25)

6. The use of the participle is extended in the reading passage. Two ablative absolute clauses are given as vocabulary items (**pecūniā datā,** 4, and **vīnō sūmptō,** 16). An explanation of this construction will be given in Chapter 42. Three of the perfect participles (**ūnctī,** 8; **tersī,** 15; and **indūtus,** 22) can be tackled in the ways suggested in Chapter 31, as can the deponent participle **ēgressus** (1). Students should be reminded that **ēgressus,** though passive in form, is active in meaning. The fact that **vestīmenta exūta** (6) is in the accusative case may cause some difficulty, but it provides an opportunity for showing yet another way of translating the perfect participle, e.g., "the clothes which had been taken off." See page 89 of the third student's book for an explanation of **lūdentibus** (24).

7. For the genitive singular **ūnīus** (25), students may be referred to the chart on page 127 of the student's book and may compare the genitive singular forms in the chart on page 130 of the student's book.

8. For the **Campus Martius** (2), see *Rome: Its People, Life and Customs,* pp. 25–26, and *Rome and Environs,* p. 95; for the **Thermae Nerōnēae** (2), see *Pictorial Dictionary of Ancient Rome,* Vol. II, pp. 460–464; for the **Balneae Palātīnae** (21), see *Rome and Environs,* map on p. 131, **Thermae**. For the emperor's freedmen (**lībertī Caesaris,** 20), see the third teacher's handbook, Chapter 27, Student's Book, note 9c.

9. Exercise 41a draws students' attention to the three different uses of the subjunctive in subordinate clauses presented in this Chapter. In No. 4, the students' will have to supply the infinitive **scīre**.

10. *VERBS: Subjunctive Mood I:* Subjunctives have been used in the course since Chapter 38 toward the end of the third student's book, and the explanation given in Chapter 39 was intended mainly to draw students' attention to the new form in such a way that it did not seem to be a new, major hurdle. It will be noted, too, that at this stage we use only the imperfect and pluperfect subjunctives. They are far more common in Latin than the other tenses, and they are also

very easily recognized because of their similarity to the present and perfect infinitives. The present and perfect subjunctives will be dealt with in Chapter 49.

Questions of terminology will inevitably be raised with the formal introduction of the subjunctive. Students are told on page 9 of the student's book that the subjunctive frequently occurs in Latin in *subordinate* clauses. Subordinate clauses should be carefully contrasted with main clauses (the English translations of the Latin examples on page 9 of the student's book are useful for this purpose); the etymology of the word *subordinate* will help (**sub-**"under" + **ordō** "order," "rank," "position," cf. *ordinal* numbers). The term *subjunctive* may then easily be explained as the form of the verb that you use when joining (**iungere**) one clause beneath (**sub-**) another. The term *subjunctive* may further be explained in contrast to *indicative*, which is a term that has not yet been formally introduced in this course but should be introduced at this time. Again, the etymology may help: **indicāre** "to point out," "to show." The indicative is thus often used in a main clause to state a fact while the subjunctive is often used in subordinate clauses. Finally, there is the term *mood*, derived from Latin **modus** "manner," "way" and English *mode* and influenced in spelling by the English word *mood* referring to the state of one's feelings. *Mood*, then, is simply the *manner* in which an action is conceived, and the concept may best be illustrated by contrasting the four Latin moods of *infinitive* (the action as an abstract idea: "to run"), the *imperative* (command: "Run!"), the *indicative* (statement of fact: "I run."), and the *subjunctive* (sometimes a statement of possibility: "I may run."). This use of the subjunctive will be studied later in the course, but it is convenient to mention it now in defining basic grammatical terms (keep in mind that the subjunctives that the students are now encountering in their reading state facts and possibilities, and the subjunctive is used in these constructions as a subordinating device and not as a means of stating a possibility).

11. *Imperfect Subjunctive:* We give the imperfect subjunctive of **esse** first in the sets of charts to show how simple it is to form this tense of the subjunctive (=infinitive + personal endings). For reinforcement, the teacher may ask students in succession around the classroom to give the imperfect subjunctive forms of the other irregular verbs and then of the deponent verbs (of which the 1st person singular forms only are given at the bottom of page 10 of the student's books).

12. *Pluperfect Subjunctive:* Again, the simplicity and regularity of the formation of these subjuctive forms should be emphasized. Students may be asked in succession to give the pluperfect subjunctive forms of the other verbs given in the sets on page 10.

13. When doing Exercise 41c, the teacher may ask in addition for students to give in English the direct question that is implied in each indirect question. Special attention should be paid to the tense of the original

question and the tense in English that is used when the indirect questions are translated from Latin.

14. *The Baths:* The note referring to separate sections in the **thermae** for men and women is true for the period of our family, but later Emperors, e.g., Hadrian, introduced separate times for men and women. For some information on the baths, see the following:
   a. *Rome: Its People, Life and Customs,* "The Baths," pp. 221–227.
   b. *Daily Life in Ancient Rome,* "The Baths," pp. 254–263.
   c. *Roman Life,* pp. 247–255 (richly illustrated).
   d. For the Baths of Diocletian, see *Rome and Environs,* pp. 189–196, and *Pictorial Dictionary of Ancient Rome,* Vol. II, pp. 448–453.
   e. For the Baths of Caracalla, see *Rome and Environs,* pp. 222–223, and *Pictorial Dictionary of Ancient Rome,* Vol. II, pp. 434–441.
   f. For appreciation of the architecture of the Roman bathing establishments, see *Roman Art and Architecture,* pp. 106–110, and *Roman Architecture,* pp. 37–38.

The Roman baths were generally well regarded as a social institution offering a wide range of benefits to the people of the city. For a very different view emphasizing the nuisance of the noise and commotion of the baths, see the letter of Seneca contained in the cultural background readings at the end of this handbook (p. 47). Seneca's letter could be used as a springboard for a debate or for written work contrasting positive and negative aspects of the baths as a public institution.

Students might also be invited to consider whether there is any counterpart to the baths in modern urban life. If not, why not? Why did the Romans develop this particular public institution, and why do modern cities not have public baths of this sort? What is lost by not having public baths? Is anything gained? To what extent do private gymnasiums, athletic clubs, health spas, and country clubs duplicate the facilities and social opportunities offered by the ancient Roman baths?

Language Activity Book

1. In Activity 41a, students may use any gender in the perfect passive participles that is consistent with the meaning of the verb.

2. In Activities 41b, c, and d, students must pay particular attention to the tenses of the verbs in the subordinate clauses. In the circumstantial and causal clauses (Activities 41b and c), a pluperfect indicative will be changed to a pluperfect subjunctive, and an imperfect indicative to an imperfect subjunctive. In each case the former indicates time before that of the main verb and the latter indicates time contemporaneous with that of the main verb.

In the indirect questions (Activity 41d), a present tense in the direct question will become an imperfect subjunctive in the indirect, and a perfect tense in the direct question will become a pluperfect in the indirect. The imperfect subjunctive indicates an action going on at the same time as that of the main verb; the pluperfect subjunctive indicates an action that took place prior to the time of the main verb. Note that in Nos. 1, 5, and 6 the 2nd person verb of the direct question becomes 3rd person in the indirect.

3. Activity 41e: An English to Latin vocabulary list for this and all other English to Latin translation exercises in the language activity book is included on pages 62–64 of this teacher's handbook. It may be duplicated and given to students as needed, and it may also be used for general English-Latin vocabulary review.

In the second sentence in Activity 41e, students may use a **cum** circumstantial clause or a perfect passive participle as in the sample below and as in line 6 of the story in the student's book. The following is a sample translation of the paragraph:

> Senex calvus tunicā russātā indūtus pecūniā datā in vestibulum thermārum iniit. Vestīmenta in apodytēriō exūta servīs trādidit. In palaestram ingressus pilā cum duōbus puerīs capillātīs lūdere coepit. Cum pilae ad terram cecidissent, eās nōn repetēbat.
>
> Cum servus adstāns follem plēnum pilārum habēret, senex diū lūdere poterat. Tandem digitōs concrepuit et vīnum poposcit. Vīnō sūmptō, senex dēfessus ad terram cecidit. Numquam rēs tam rīdiculōsa vīsa est!

CHAPTER 42: STOP THIEF!

Student's Book

1. **a.** This chapter continues the presentation of the use of the perfect passive participle begun in Chapter 31 and discusses the ablative absolute (two examples of which have already occurred in 41:4 and 16).
   b. The story shifts to Marcus and Sextus and their adventures in the baths on the way home from school.

2. **a.** Students should have no trouble with the perfect passive participles in the nominative case modifying the subject of the sentence (used since Chapter 31). Examples are **ēgressī** (1, 5), **lāpsus** (25), and **captus** (27). The perfect participles of deponent verbs are, of course, active in meaning (page 65 of the third student's book).
   b. It is hoped that students will be able to use the translation supplied for the ablative absolute **quibus verbīs audītīs** (3) to help them deal with **vestīmentīs exūtīs** (6), **vestīmentīs trāditīs** (13), and **Sextō vīsō** (24), but they may need some help from the teacher. The meaning of the more difficult ablative absolute without a participle (**mē custōde**, 12) is supplied. It is recommended that the passage be completed before attempting explanations of the ablative absolute constructions.

   c. With the exception of the two ablative absolutes in Chapter 41, the perfect passive participle has not been used previously in cases other than the nominative (except in the exercises in the language activity book for Chapter 31). The story in Chapter 42 includes three examples in the accusative case. Students may translate **vestīmenta surrepta** (9–10) as "the stolen clothes," but other translations (see Chapter 31, pages 34–35) are possible, such as ". . . thieves who *steal clothes and* sell them in the city." Literal translations of the perfect passive participles **cōnspectum** (24) and **captum** (28) may be given ("having been seen"; "having been caught"), but smoother English translations as coordinate or subordinate clauses should be encouraged, e.g., "Sextus, however, saw the thief and began to follow him," and "When Sextus caught him, he handed him over to his master."

3. **Structures:**
   a. Linking **quī** (see note on pages 20–21 of the student's book):
   Quibus verbīs audītīs, ... (3)
   Cui Asellus respondit, ... (11)
   Quod ubi vīdit. . . . (19)
   Quem captum. . . . (27–28)
   b. Anaphora: **Simul fūr . . ., simul Asellus . . . , simul Sextus. . . .** (19–20)

4. Treat **exeāmus** (6) as a vocabulary item. This use of the subjunctive will be discussed in the fifth student's book.

   Note the dative **alterī** (8), clued by **servō**; if students ask about the form, they may be told that **alter** declines as does **ūnus** (chart on page 127 of the student's book). Compare the dative singulars of **ille** and **is**.

5. Lines 13–16 are suitable for dictation.

6. *VERBS: Perfect Passive Participles:* This section continues the discussion begun in the note with the same title on page 34 of the third student's book. The teacher may wish to review that note and the comments in the third teacher's handbook, Chapter 31, Student's Book, note 2, and Language Activity Book, note 1.

   In the example with the dative case we have introduced the idiom **gratiās agere**, which will be met in Chapter 50.

7. *VERBS: Ablative Absolute:* The ablative absolute is a clause separate from the rest of the sentence in the sense that its subject cannot be the same as the subject, direct object, or indirect object of the main clause. This means that ablative absolutes could not be substituted for the boldface words in the examples on page 18 of the student's book. One could not, for example, say:
   Coquō vocātō, ab omnibus laudātus est.
   The cook having been summoned, *he was praised by all.*

When the subject, direct object, or indirect object of the subordinate and main clauses would be the same, the simple participle is used, as in the examples on page 18 of the student's book.

The tenses of the participles in ablative absolutes indicate both *time* and *aspect* of the action. The present participle indicates an action *continuing* at the *same* time as the action of the main verb (see page 90 of the third student's book); the perfect participle indicates an action *completed* at some time *before* that of the main verb (see page 35 of the third student's book).

8. In the light of the observation in the first paragraph of note 7 above, it may be observed that the participles in Exercise 42c could not be replaced with ablative absolutes and that the ablative absolutes in Exercise 42d could not be incorporated into the main clauses as simple participles. Students should become aware of the fact that the ablative absolute is a clause unrelated grammatically to the structure of the main clause. Compare Exercise 42c, No. 8, with Exercise 42d, No. 8. In Exercise 42c, No. 7, **prōcēdere** is to be deduced.

9. *The Difficulty of Guarding Clothes at the Baths:* Most of the Latin will be easily understood by students at this level. For suggestions on handling passages such as this that are given in both Latin and English, see the third teacher's handbook, Chapter 28, Student's Book, note 12b. The following vocabulary may prove useful:

> **quippe quī,** since he
> **fallō, fallere** (3), **fefellī, falsum,** to deceive, (passive) to be mistaken, confused

10. **Versiculī**: "The Thief's Accomplice," page 117 Students may have trouble with the inverted **malus quis,** "What evil (man) . . . ?" The **somnifer deus** is Mercury, god of thieves, whose wand induces sleep (Ovid, *Metamorphoses*, I.671–672).

Language Activity Book

1. Activity 42a gives practice with perfect passive participles used in a variety of cases in the sentences. The sets of sentences show how perfect passive participles may be regarded as reduced forms of full sentences.

2. Activity 42b gives practice with the forms and the translation of present participles. Note that the present participles will often be translated with the continuous past tense in English. A different translation for No. 5 is possible if the main verb is interpreted as present ("Euclides *says*") rather than past. In No. 9, **ā** could mean either "from" or "by"; the former meaning is required by the sense of the sentence.

3. In Activity 42c, students should be alert to the fact that the imperfect indicative verbs in the first sentences in the sets will become *present* participles in the ablative absolutes to indicate continuous actions taking place at the same time as those of the main verbs. Perfect tenses in the first sentences in the sets will become perfect participles to indicate actions that were completed before the actions of the main verbs.

4. The answers given in the teacher's edition for Activity 42d are only suggestions of possible answers and are not exhaustive. Students may be interested to learn that the words having *-pris* instead of *(-)pre-* came into English by way of French, in which the past participle of *prendre* is *pris*.

CHAPTER 43: PYRAMUS AND THISBE

Student's Book

1. **a.** This chapter provides consolidation of the uses of the participles met so far and introduces the future active participle.
   b. The scene at the baths provides an excuse by way of a quotation from Martial (III.44) for the telling of one of the most famous short stories from the ancient world. Extracts from the telling of the story by Ovid are included in the language activity book as the first extended reading of real Latin in the course. An English translation of Ovid's version of the story is included in the cultural background readings at the end of this handbook. Geoffrey Chaucer (*c.* 1343–1400) drew from Ovid in his retelling of the story of Pyramus and Thisbe ("The Legend of Thisbe, of Babylon, the Martyr") in his *The Lengend of Good Women*, which includes nine stories of ancient heroines and introduced the heroic couplet into English verse. William Shakespeare (1564–1616) incorporated the story of Pyramus and Thisbe as a play within a play in Act V of *A Midsummer Night's Dream*. This highly dramatic and mawkish parody, full of alliteration, pathos, and verbal humor may be compared with the classical restraint of Ovid's version. Students who have read Shakespeare's romantic tragedy, *Romeo and Juliet*, will be interested in discovering similarities of plot and characterization to the Pyramus and Thisbe story. Comparisons of Ovid and Shakespeare may provide opportunities for discussion and written work, and students may also be invited to try their hands at creative writing projects based on themes in the Pyramus and Thisbe story but set in the students' contemporary world. Leonard Bernstein's *West Side Story* could provide an example.

2. Words to be deduced: **commūnis** (7), **sēcrētō** (9), **leō** (15), **prope** (adverb; 16), **sanguineus** (17), **noctū** (21), and **lacrima** (25). Form to be deduced: **Thisbēn** (6).

3. Participles:
   a. Present active: **amantibus** (8), **sedentēs** (9), **exprimēns** (9), **tremēns** (20), **moriēns** (23), and

iacēns (25: note accusative neuter, modifying **corpus**).

b. Perfect, nominative case: **vīsa** (8), **ēgressa** (14), **ēgressus** (18), and **commōtī** (29).

c. Perfect, accusative case: **cōnspectam** (3) and **aspersum** (19).

d. Ablative absolutes: **Pȳramō vīsō** (3–4), **ōsculīs mūrō datīs** (10), **ōre sanguine bovis aspersō** (15), **Quō cōnspectō** (15), **Gladiō igitur strictō** (22), **Metū nōndum dēpositō** (24), and **suō vēlāmine cōnspectō** (26).

e. Note ablative absolute without participle: **parentibus īnsciīs** (11–12).

f. Future active: **moritūra** (27).

4. Structures:

a. Interrupted sentences:
Parentēs. . . , quoniam. . . rixābantur, eōs. . . . (4–5)
. . . Thisbē . . . , cum . . . cēlāvisset, fūrtim ēgressa ad silvam festīnāvit. (13–14)
. . . Pȳramus ex urbe ēgressus, dum . . . progreditur, vestīgia. . . . (18–19)

b. Participial phrases: Note how occasionally in participial phrases other words are introduced between the noun/pronoun and the participle in order to build up the students' ability to handle more complicated phrases: **virginem in viā forte cōnspectam** (3), **ōre sanguine bovis aspersō** (15), **vēlāmen sanguine aspersum** (19), **gladiō igitur strictō** (22), **metū nōndum dēpositō** (24), and **corpus eius humī iacēns** (25).

c. Linking **quī**:
Quam ad rīmam. . . . (8)
Quō cum advēnisset, ... (14)
Quō cōnspectō, ... (15)
Quod vēlāmen. . . . (17)

d. List: **Cōnstituērunt . . . exīre, . . . convenīre, . . . cōnsīdere.** (11–13)

e. Emphatic position: **moriēns** (23)

f. Inverted word order: **multīs cum lacrimīs** (25)

5. Various minor points of grammar and style:

a. For **domō** (2) as a 2nd declension ablative singular of a 4th declension noun, see the third teacher's handbook, Chapter 37, Student's Book, note 10.

b. Note the different uses of **et** in the first paragraph: **Et Thisbē. . . .** (3), "Thisbe also. . . ."; and **. . . et . . . et. . . .** (4), " . . . both . . . and . . . ."

c. **quoniam multōs iam annōs . . . rixābantur** (4–5): "since they had then been quarreling for many years." The imperfect indicative with **iam** and an expression of duration of time indicates an action that had been taking place and was still continuing at the time of the action of the main verb.

d. The **-n** of the Greek accusative ending of **Thisbēn** (6) has been met in the third language activity book (Chapters 36 and following) in the word

Aenēān and should cause students no problem here.

e. Note the datives **utrīque** (7) and **alterī** (9); see above, Chapter 42, Student's Book, note 4.

f. **silentiō noctis** (13): ablative of time when.

g. **dum fugit** (16) and **dum . . . progreditur** (18–19): Students should be reminded that the present tense in Latin in this construction will be translated with an imperfect in English, e.g., "while she was fleeing."

h. **Noctū** (21), as if from a 4th declension noun, is an alternative for **nocte** (12); there is no difference in meaning.

6. *VERBS: Future Active Participles:* The **-ūr-** which appears in all forms of the future active participles can be easily remembered from the English word *future*, itself derived from the future active participle of the Latin verb **esse** (given in Note 4 on page 25 of the student's book).

Note the different layouts for the regular verbs and the deponents. This is intended to help students remember the active/passive and form/meaning differences. The verb **orior**, which is used as an example of participles of 4th conjugation verbs on page 25, will be introduced in Exercise 43b on the next page, but students have met **coorior** in 40:3–4. Cf. the English *orient* (and *occident*).

For the declension of the present active participle, see the chart on page 129 of the student's book; the perfect and future participles are, of course, declined as 1st and 2nd declension adjectives (see page 126 of the student's book).

7. *The Fine Art of Poetry:* Horace's use of the future participle **scrīptūrus** suggests an additional possible meaning (see note 5 on page 25 of the student's book) for this tense of the participle; "hoping to. . . ."

8. *Lovers' Graffiti:* These graffiti, included to give a more mundane view of love in the ancient world to contrast with that of Pyramus and Thisbe, are mostly from *Roman Voices: Everyday Latin in Ancient Rome* and the *Teacher's Guide* to the same (Chapter Four). The second line of No. VI could have been addressed to the parents of Pyramus and Thisbe.

9. **Versiculī:** "A Difference of Opinion," page 117 The poem reflects a standing dispute between Cornelia and the rough-and-tumble Sextus over the power of romantic love as illustrated in the story of Pyramus and Thisbe. Note the emphatic repetition of **tē** in the first line. To be deduced: **vēmenter** (3) equals **vehementer**, and **sānus** (4).

Language Activity Book

1. The following are sample translations (fairly literal to show the structure of the Latin) of the passages from Ovid:

Pyramus and Thisbe, the one the most handsome of young men, the other excelling (all the other) girls that the Orient possessed, had adjacent homes, where Semiramis is said to have surrounded her tall city with walls of sun-baked bricks.

And Babylonian Thisbe saw it far off under the rays of the moon, and she fled with timid foot into a dark cave, and while she fled, her veil slipped off her back and she left it (on the ground).

Pyramus when indeed he also found the veil (now) stained with blood, said, "One night will destroy two lovers, of whom she was most worthy of a long life; my soul is guilty. I have destroyed you, pitiable woman, I who ordered that you should come at night into places full of fear and I did not come here first (myself).

"Pyramus," she shouted, "what accident has taken you away from me? Pyramus, reply! Your dearest Thisbe calls you by name; listen and lift your head (that is) lying (on the ground)!" At the (mention of) Thisbe's name, Pyramus raised his eyes (that were) weighted down by death, and upon seeing her he closed them again.

"I will follow you in death, and I will be said (to have been) the most wretched cause and companion of your death; and you who were able to be torn away from me by death alone will not be able to be torn away by death."

Her prayers touched the gods, they touched their parents; for the color on the fruit, when it fully ripens, is black, and what remains from the funeral pyres rests in one urn.

WORD STUDY XI

1. The aims of this Word Study section are:
   a. to explain Latin diminutive suffixes on nouns and adjectives
   b. to explain the formation and meaning of Latin frequentative verbs
   c. to present English derivatives of Latin frequentative verbs and diminutive nouns and adjectives.

2. In order to simplify presentation of diminutives, discussion is limited to noun and adjective bases. Verb bases are also used in diminutives, e.g., **spectāculum** (**spectō**).

3. If clarification of the function of diminutive suffixes is needed, the point could be made that the same function is achieved in English by the suffixes *-let* (booklet), *-kin* (lambkin), *-ling* (duckling), and a borrowing from French, *-ette* or *-et* (statuette, puppet).

4. Exercise 1 illustrates the range of meanings that are possible with diminutive suffixes, e.g.:

   smallness: **lapillus, oppidulum, lectulus, libellus, cistella, capitulum**

youth: **servulus, ancillula** (**ancilla** itself is a diminutive of **ancula**, *slave girl*), **puellula** (**puella** itself is a diminutive of **puer**)

disparagement: **servulus**, *worthless slave*; **muliercula**, *weak* or *foolish woman*

affection: **amīcula**, *mistress* or *girlfriend*

special meaning: **libellus**, *notebook, pamphlet, document, placard, program*; **capitulum**, *person* (used in plays), *flower bud, point* (of an implement), *column capital, hemorrhoid* (!)

5. Some students may be curious about certain Latin words they have met that have the **-ulus** (**-a**, **-um**) suffix with no obvious diminutive connotation. These may be included among those words in which the suffix provides a special or unique meaning (e.g., **ōsculum**). Further examples are:

   a. nouns with verb bases: **cubiculum** (**cubāre**, *to recline*), **vehiculum** (**vehere**, *to carry*), **spectāculum** (**spectāre**), **ferculum** (**ferre**), **iēntāculum** (**iēntāre**, *to have breakfast*; **iēiūnus**, *hungry*)
   b. nouns of Greek origin: **perīculum** (*peira*, trial), **epistula** (*epistole*, message), **baculum** (*baktron*, stick)

6. The nickname Caligula ("Bootikins"), referred to in Exercise 3, was a term of affection given to the Emperor Gaius as a boy by the soldiers of his father Germanicus; the story may be found in both Suetonius (*Caligula* 9) and Tacitus (*Annals* I.41).

7. Although Exercises 4, 5, and 6 on frequentative (intensive, iterative) verbs are intended mainly to enhance students' vocabulary in Latin, English derivatives of these and other frequentative verbs are worthy of note. English derivatives are commonly made from the supine stems of Latin frequentative verbs, according to the principles discussed in Word Study VI, e.g., *dictate, hesitate, agitate, gestate*.

8. Exercise 5 encourages students to explore the contrast between those frequentatives whose meanings are closely identified with the meanings of the original verbs (e.g., **iactō**, from **iaciō**) and those frequentatives whose meanings are more radically changed by the addition of the suffix (e.g., **habitō**, from **habeō**). Students should be urged to be flexible in accepting this seemingly ambivalent function of frequentative suffixes and to approach each new frequentative verb with caution, checking a dictionary to confirm their conjectures as to its meaning.

REVIEW X

Student's Book

1. The main grammatical features in Chapters 41—43 that require review are:
   a. the forms of the imperfect and pluperfect subjunctives (regular, deponent, and irregular verbs)

b. the use of the subjunctive in circumstantial and causal clauses and indirect questions

c. uses of the perfect participle

d. the ablative absolute (with both present and perfect participles)

e. linking **quī**

f. the future active participle

2. In Exercise Xa, **trānsgredī** (2) and **Gallī** (3, 4) are to be deduced. Students should produce "the Britains also" for **et Britannī** (3) from the occurrence of **Et Thisbē** "Thisbe also" in 43:3.

3. In connection with Exercise Xb, teachers may invite discussion of style by asking for preferences between the construction used in the passage and the correct alternative construction in Exercise Xb. What are the strengths or weaknesses of each alternative construction?

4. In Exercise Xc, **sine discrīmine** (2), **adīre** (4), **magnificus** (9), and **incurrere** (13) are to be deduced. It may be well to remind students of the future perfect indicative (**invēneris,** 5) and its use in future conditions.

For the full story of the Sabine women, see Livy, I.9−13. The Sabine women were reconciled to their new husbands as follows:

> Romulus himself went among them and explained that the pride of their parents had caused this deed, when they had refused their neighbors the right to intermarry; nevertheless the daughters should be wedded and become co-partners in all the possessions of the Romans, in their citizenship and, dearest privilege of all to the human race, in their children; only let them moderate their anger, and give their hearts to those to whom fortune had given their persons. A sense of injury had often given place to affection, and they would find their husbands the kinder for this reason, that every man would earnestly endeavor not only to be a good husband, but also to console his wife for the home and parents she had lost. His arguments were seconded by the wooing of the men, who excused their act on the score of passion and love, the most moving of all pleas to a woman's heart. (I.9)

The Sabine parents of the seized women, however, did not accept the situation, and the Sabines attacked Rome. After various fortunes of battle and at a moment when the Sabine leader had fled and the Romans had gained the advantage, the Sabine wives of the Romans intervened between the two warring forces:

> Then the Sabine women, whose wrong had given rise to the war, with loosened hair and torn garments, their woman's timidity lost in a sense of their misfortune, dared to go among the flying missiles, and rushing in from the side, to part the hostile forces and disarm them of their anger, beseeching their fathers on this side, on that their

> husbands, that fathers-in-law and sons-in-law should not stain themselves with impious bloodshed, nor pollute with parricide the suppliants' children, grandsons to one party and sons to the other. "If you regret," they continued, "the relationship that unites you, if you regret the marriage-tie, turn your anger against us; we are the cause of war, the cause of wounds, and even death to both our husbands and our parents. It will be better for us to perish than to live, lacking either of you, as widows or as orphans." It was a touching plea, not only to the rank and file, but to their leaders as well. A stillness fell on them, and a sudden hush. Then the leaders came forward to make a truce, and not only did they agree on peace, but they made one people out of the two. They shared the sovereignty, but all authority was transferred to Rome. In this way the population was doubled, and that some concession might after all be granted the Sabines, the citizens were named Quirites, from the town of Cures. (I.13)

> —tr. B.O. Foster

Language Activity Book

The following are sample translations of the sentences in RXa:

1. Cum Rōmulus plūrimōs praedōnēs et aliōs scelestōs hominēs in urbem accēpisset, penūria mulierum inventa est.

2. Cum virī īrātī essent, ad Rōmulum adiērunt.

3. Virī cognōscere cupiēbant quōmodo uxōrēs invenīre possent.

4. Vīcīnī populī nūntiōs ā Rōmulō missōs nōn cōmiter accēpērunt.

5. Lūdīs magnificīs Neptūnō parātīs, Rōmulus omnēs Sabīnōs cum līberīs et uxōribus invītāvit.

6. Sabīnīs sedentibus et spectāculum spectantibus, Rōmulus signum virīs Rōmānīs dedit.

7. Cum Rōmānī in multitūdinem spectātōrum incurrerent, fēminae Sabīnae magnā vōce clāmāvērunt.

8. Rōmulus Rōmānōs fīliās Sabīnōrum adortōs et in urbem trahentēs laudāvit.

9. Rōmānī fīliās Sabīnōrum uxōrēs habitūrī laetī erant.

10. Quae nūptiīs celebrātīs quoque laetae erant.

CHAPTER 44: A RAINY DAY

Student's Book

1. a. This chapter begins our formal treatment of the accusative and infinitive in indirect statement. It also includes a tabulation of the forms of the irregular verb **fīō**.

b. The readings in the Chapter deal with games played by the Romans. For more information on this subject, see "Sports and Pastimes of Children and Adults," pp. 232−242 in *Rome:*

Its People, Life and Customs and the treatments in *Roman Life,* pp. 241–245, and *Daily Life in Ancient Rome,* pp. 251–252.

2. Words to be deduced: **referre** (24) and **ēdūcere** (28).

3. The syntactical structure of the reading passage has been kept fairly simple in order to make it easier to introduce some examples of the accusative and infinitive in indirect statements. There are six in all; five of them depend on **putō:**

patrem esse crūdēlem (4)
hunc lūdum esse optimum (8)
hunc lūdum esse pessimum (10)
vōs esse molestissimōs hodiē (15)
patrem in animō habēre Sextum verberāre (30)

A sixth depends on **crēdis:**

mē pūpā lūdere (20)

It will be noted that all of the introductory verbs and the infinitives are in the present tense. From a literal translation such as "I think father to be cruel" (4), it should be possible for students to move to the more natural "I think that. . . ." We strongly recommend that teachers should, at least in the early stages, emphasize the use of the hinge word "that"; it may not seem necessary with the early, straightforward examples, but it will be a particularly useful cue word when dealing with more complicated examples of indirect statement, particularly those depending on a main verb in secondary sequence.

Teachers should also point out that Latin does not use a *separate* word for "that." In English, "that" is frequently a clue for indirect statement, whereas in Latin the change to the accusative and infinitive is the clue. The examples in *Accusative and Infinitive (Indirect Statement) I* (page 36 of the student's book) are set forth to illustrate this, but the actual verbalization of the point will emphasize it even more for the students. Otherwise there will be students who will try to put in a relative pronoun for the hinge word "that," or a form of **is** or **ille.**

4. The passage contains a number of other infinitives in constructions that may be contrasted with the examples of indirect statement tabulated above:

"Ego in animō habēbam . . . **dēscendere** et . . . **īre** . . . ." (2–3)
" . . . pater nōs domī **manēre** iussit." (3–4)
"In palaestram **īre** cupiēbāmus. . . ." (6)
"Ego vōs docēbō latrunculīs **lūdere.**" (7–8)
"Nōnne vīs pār impār **lūdere** vel digitīs **micāre?**" (11)
Statim **clāmāre** coepērunt ambō. (12)
"Nōlīte clāmōribus vestrīs **vexāre** mātrem et Cornēliam!" (14–15)
"Nōlī nōs **vexāre!**" (18)
"Nōlī pūpam **laedere!**" (24)
" . . . patrem in animō habēre Sextum **verberāre.**" (30)

These uses of the infinitive should be carefully noted

alongside of the accusative and infinitive construction for indirect statement, and they may be categorized as follows:

    a. complementary infinitive: 2–3, 6, 11, 12, 30
    b. complementary infinitive with **nōlī** or **nōlīte** to express a negative imperative: 14–15, 18, 24
    c. accusative and infinitive after **iubēre, docēre:** 3–4, 7–8

5. The passage also provides reinforcement of ablative absolutes (e.g., **clāmōribus audītīs,** 16, and **pūpā abreptā,** 23), including the phrases **quō vīsō** (23) and **quō factō** (29), which should almost become stock vocabulary items.

6. Notes on vocabulary:
    a. Bonō animō este! (7): Literally, "Be of a good spirit!" (abl. of description)
    b. lūdus (8): The word is new in the sense of "a game." Compare **lūdī, -ōrum** *(m pl),* games (as in the Circus Maximus; cf. 23:15).
    c. ambō (12) is declined like **duo** (see page 127 of the student's book). Derivatives: *ambidextrous, ambience, ambiguous, ambivalent.*
    d. pāreō (16) takes the dative case: = "be subject *to,*" "be obedient *to.*"
    e. Num . . . ? (19): Compare **Nōnne . . . ?** See the second teacher's handbook, Chapter 18, Student's Book, note 5.
    f. dōnō dare (21): The noun **dōnō** is dative of purpose "for (or "as") a gift." Be sure that students do not think of **dōnō** as a verb in the 1st person singular or a dative of indirect object.
    g. peristȳlium (23) is a Greek word transliterated into Latin, as were the names of several parts of houses and estates. The letter *y* transliterates the Greek *upsilon; peri-* is Greek for "around," and *stylus* is Greek for "pillar" or "column."
    h. Quid Sextō fīet? (29): "What will happen to Sextus?" "What will become of Sextus?" This idiom is used with either the dative or the ablative case.

7. Students may usefully be asked to locate in the passage subordinate clauses with verbs in the subjunctive and to identify the type of clause and the tense of the subjunctive in each case (17 and 25–26 contain indirect questions with their verbs in the imperfect and pluperfect, respectively, and 25 contains a circumstantial clause with its verb in the pluperfect).

8. Lines 14–17 are suitable for dictation and will require sensitivity to an indirect statement, an ablative absolute, and an indirect question.

9. Exercise 44a gives practice with the various uses of the infinitive (see 3 and 4 above). Some teachers may wish to delay doing this exercise until after dealing with the language note on page 36 and Exercises 44b and c.

10. *Accusative and Infinitive (Indirect Statement) I:* In dealing with the sentences used as illustrations in this

note, it may be useful to distinguish between direct and indirect statements and to ask the students in each case, "What was the direct statement?" They will then see that the indirect statement with the infinitive is a transformation of a direct statement with the indicative (in these examples). Awareness of this will prepare them for Activity 44b in the language activity book.

The use of the reflexive pronoun in the example **Sextus sentit sē aegrum esse** will be dealt with in the next chapter.

11. Exercise 44b gives practice with a variety of main verbs, all of them in the present tense, followed by accusatives and infinitives in which the infinitives are all present tense. This exercise should help to reinforce the value in English translation of the hinge word "that."

12. Exercise 44c draws particular attention to the fact that the subject of the indirect statement and any adjective agreeing with its subject are in the accusative case. In No. 7, **merīdiēs** is to be deduced.

13. *Games Played by Children and Adults:* The first passage is from a poem on the walnut tree. The poem is contained in the works of Ovid but is thought not to be by him. Most of the couplets are self-contained in thought, and we present them here with translations in between. Students should be able to make many connections between the Latin and the English. We recommend that each couplet be treated individually with one student reading the translation aloud first and then another student reading the Latin. As the students are then invited to figure out exactly how each of the games described is played, the teacher should focus attention on the Latin words and their meaning so that the students will be painlessly translating the Latin while figuring out how each game was played.

The "heavenly constellation" (fifth couplet) is a triangular group of stars near Aries, and the fourth letter in the Greek alphabet is *delta*.

14. *The Irregular Verb* **fīō, fierī, factus sum:** It should be mentioned that the perfect, pluperfect, and future perfect are formed regularly: **factus sum, factus eram,** and **factus erō**.

15. *Versiculī:* "Sextus Reproved," page 118
In line 2, **puellāris** is to be deduced. The passive periphrastic **ferenda (est)** should be treated as a vocabulary item; it is, as usual, accompanied by a dative (rather than ablative) of personal agent (**tibi** modified by the phrase **annōs tot . . . nātō**).

16. *Circus and Arena:* For further background information on holidays and games, see *Daily Life in Ancient Rome*, pp. 202–206.

Language Activity Book

1. Activity 44b is designed to help students see the relationship between direct and indirect statements. The direct statement is given, and the student is to convert it into an indirect statement. Students may need help producing **ad sē** to replace **ad puerōs** in No. 6.

2. The following is a sample translation of the paragraph in Activity 44d (students may need to locate the Latin word for "quietly" in the English-Latin vocabulary list):

Quid Cānō fit? Prīnceps eum necārī iussit, sed dīcunt eum sollicitum nōn esse. Omnēs sciunt eum etiam cum custōdibus latrunculīs placidē lūdere et calculōs numerāre. Custōdēs crēdunt Cānum vincere, etiam ad mortem progredientem.

CHAPTER 45: LOOKING FORWARD TO THE GAMES

Student's Book

1. a. This chapter extends the student's experience with the accusative and infinitive construction in indirect statements by introducing examples with future and perfect infinitives, all in the active voice and after main verbs in the present tense.

Examples with future infinitives:

tē crās nōn labōrātūrum esse (5)
tē quoque ad mūnera itūrum esse (6–7)
Aurēliam eō nōn itūram esse (18)
nōs tē in amphitheātrō vīsūrōs esse (26–27)

Examples with perfect infinitives:

mē per iocum hoc dīxisse (11)
Iūdaeōs dīligenter labōrāvisse et amphitheātrum . . . cōnfēcisse (12–13)

The future infinitive will be formally taught after the reading passage. Students will most likely identify it in the course of the reading. Insertion of the word "that" when translating indirect statements will provide a useful cue.

b. In addition to the use of future and perfect infinitives in indirect statements, the use of **sē** and **eum** in these constructions is treated in this chapter.

c. Forms of the so-called future active periphrastic (e.g., **itūrī sunt,** 6) are introduced in this chapter (other examples in lines 20 and 23). They will cause students no problem since they may be translated literally ("they are about to go"). Simple future indicatives may be substituted for these periphrastic constructions, but the periphrastic construction does offer the additional meanings of *intention* or *likelihood*.

d. This is the first of four chapters on the Colosseum and gladiatorial and other combats that took place there. The theme of the stories thus moves from recreation (baths and poetry, Chapters 41–43) and children's games (Chap-

ter 44) to games of life and death in the arena—
which had a compelling, fascination for the
Romans.

    e. There is cultural background on the construction and dedication of the Colosseum, and the chapter ends with a presentation of the forms of the irregular verb **mālō**.

2. Words to be deduced: **memorābilis** (12) and **congredī** (17).

3. Structures:
    a. Note the emphatic position of **novum** in line 10.
    b. Balance:

        Nōs templum . . . dēlēvimus, illī amphitheātrum aedificāvērunt. . . . (13–14). Also note the emphatic position of **nostrum** at the end of the sentence.

4. **quid dīcam** (10): Although students have not as yet been introduced to the present subjunctive, it is not anticipated that this clause will cause any difficulty, especially since it echoes **Quid dīcis . . . ?** (8) uttered by Cornelius.

5. **Quō maior populus, eō plūs perīculī** (22): For this form of comparison, it may be useful to recall **Quō celerius currēbat ille, eō celerius currēbant hominēs** (34:20–21). For the quotation from Seneca, see note 8e below.

6. **est cōnficienda** (27): Treat this use of the gerundive in a passive periphrastic construction as a vocabulary item at this stage and resist the temptation to analyze and discuss it. Several other examples will be introduced in this book before an explanation is given in the fifth student's book.

7. Note the formal plurals used by Titus in his leave-taking: **"Nōs abitūrī tē salūtāmus!"** Titus undoubtedly intends a humorous parody of the gladiators' salute to the Emperor as they enter the arena: **Nōs moritūrī tē salūtāmus** (a variant is quoted by Suetonius and on page 49 of the student's book: **Moritūrī tē salūtant**).

8. Background
    a. Caesar (9) Students should realize that this is an imperial title and does not refer to Julius Caesar (see Teacher's Handbook 2, Chapter 24, Student's Book, note 5f). Augustus adopted the cognomen **Caesar** as well as the title **prīnceps** or "first citizen." Both titles were used by and in referring to other emperors as well (see, for example, 7:13). According to Dio Cassius (57.8.2), the Emperor Tiberius said of himself, "I am **dominus** of my slaves, **imperātor** of my soldiers, and **prīnceps** of the rest." Most of the Emperors after Tiberius preferred the title **Caesar**. Augustus and Tiberius had been at pains to suggest that they were ordinary Romans; later Emperors gave up that pretense.
    b. For the Colosseum and its completion and

dedication in A.D. 80, see the background notes on pages 45–46 and 48 of the student's book. The epigrams of Martial quoted there should be read in conjunction with the story here as illustrations of the pride of the Romans in the new amphitheater as one of the wonders of the world and of the arrival of people from all over the known world to celebrate its opening.

    c. Iūdaeōs (12): Jerusalem was first captured by the Romans in 63 B.C., when Pompey reduced it after a siege of three months, but the area was not annexed as a province (Judaea) until A.D. 6. Even then, the Jews were allowed freedom to control all matters pertaining to their religion, but civil affairs were the responsibility of the Roman governor. Thus, the Chief Priest, when he wanted the death penalty imposed on Christ, had to bring him before the Roman governor, Pontius Pilate. There was continuing unrest and discontent, however, provoked by tactlessness and inefficiency on the part of many of the Roman governors. In A.D. 70, the Jews rebelled against the Romans, but the revolt was ruthlessly crushed by Titus, who was to become Emperor in A.D. 79. He completely destroyed the city and the Temple, except for part of a wall that still survives as an object of profound veneration, the Western Wall. The Arch of Titus in Rome, which was dedicated by Domitian in A.D. 81 after Titus' death and still stands at the eastern end of the Roman Forum, commemorates Titus' victory over Jerusalem and pictures, in relief, the seven-branched candlestick taken from the Temple. (See *Rome and Environs*, p. 124, and *Pictorial Dictionary of Ancient Rome*, Vol. I, pp. 132–135.) Even today many Jews will not walk under the Arch of Titus because of what it symbolizes. Thousands of Jewish prisoners were brought to Rome and used as slave-labor to build the Colosseum. For further information on relations between the Jews and the Romans, including positive aspects, see Michael Grant, *The Jews in the Roman World* (New York, Scribners, 1973, now out of print but available in many libraries).

    d. togam virīlem (21): See Chapter 50.

    e. Seneca (22), the famous Stoic philosopher and advisor to Nero, was often quoted for his pithy sayings and carefully phrased **sententiae**. The quotation here is adapted from a sentence in Seneca's seventh moral epistle, in which he recommends avoiding crowds because their influence can be detrimental to one's character and peace of mind. In this letter Seneca especially inveighs against joining the crowds at the amphitheater. The paragraph containing the quoted **sententia** is given in English translation in the cultural background readings on page 50 at the end of this handbook. Another paragraph from the same letter is quoted in Latin and in English translation on page 66 of the student's book.

9. *Accusative and Infinitive (Indirect Statement) II:* While discussing this material with the students it may be well to review the formation of the perfect active infinitive (presented in Chapter 40) and of the future active participle (presented in Chapter 43). Students may usefully be reminded that the perfect active infinitive has no inflexions.

Students should become aware of the distinction between **sē** and **eum** as used in indirect statements; the point need not be labored, however, since in most reading contexts there is no ambiguity.

10. Exercise 45b is intended to give students practice in finding the appropriate English to translate the future and perfect infinitives. Note that the perfect infinitive will sometimes require the "has done" translation and sometimes the "-ed" form of the past tense.

11. Exercise 45c concentrates on two things:
    a. agreement of the future infinitive with the subject of the accusative
    b. use of clues such as **crās, paucīs diēbus,** and **heri** to anticipate what the tense of the infinitive will be. Note that in No. 3 **tē** may be either masculine or feminine; students should justify their choice of **-um** or **-am.** In No. 9, unwary students may be caught by the inverted order **respondent servī;** this could provide a useful lesson on the importance of case endings.

12. *The Colosseum:* Colosseum was the medieval name given to the **Amphitheātrum Flāvium,** which was built near the huge statue of Nero, called the **Colossus Nerōnis** because it reminded people of the Colossus of Rhodes. The name Colosseum first appears in the writings of the Venerable Bede (*c.* A.D. 673–735), who quotes the following pilgrim's proverb or prophecy (see the second student's book, page 53, and the second teacher's handbook, Chapter 22, Student's Book, note 7):

    Quam diū stat Colyssaeus, stābit et Rōma.
    Quandō cadet Colyssaeus, cadet et Rōma.
    Quandō cadet Rōma, cadet et mundus.

    While stands the Coliseum, Rome shall stand;
    When falls the Coliseum, Rome shall fall;
    And when Rome falls—the World.
                    —Lord Byron

The Flavian amphitheater was mentioned in Chapter 24 (lines 20–21), and teachers may wish to review the notes in the second teacher's handbook, Chapter 24, Student's Book, notes 5e and g, and the references given there. See also *The Colosseum* by Peter Quennell and the Editors of the Newsweek Book Division, Newsweek, New York, 1971. This book is out of print but may be found in some libraries. It gives a full and marvelously illustrated account of the Colosseum in antiquity and through the ages. Finding a copy of it will be worth the effort.

Construction of the building was undertaken by Vespasian between A.D. 70 and 76 on the site of the artificial lake created by Nero as part of the gardens of his **Domus Aurea.** Martial records the delight of the Roman people over the dismantling of the **Domus Aurea** and the construction on its site of new buildings of use to the Roman people (second epigram on page 48 of the student's book).

Suetonius (*Titus* VII) describes Titus' dedication of the amphitheater as follows:

> [Titus] was second to none of his predecessors in munificence. At the dedication of the amphitheater and of the baths which were hastily built near it he gave a most magnificent and costly gladiatorial show. He presented a sham sea-fight too in the old naumachia, and in the same place a combat of gladiators, exhibiting five thousand wild beasts of every kind in a single day.
>   —tr. J.C. Rolfe

13. *The Irregular Verb* **mālō, mālle, māluī:** In addition to the epigram of Martial, the following **sententiae** from Sallust may be used:

    Esse quam vidērī bonus mālēbat.
    He (Cato) wanted to be rather than (merely) to seem (to be) virtuous. (Bellum Catilinae LIV.6)
    Optimus quisque facere māvult quam dīcere.
    All the best men prefer doing to talking. (Bellum Catilinae VIII.5)

14. *Martial,* **De spectaculis:** notes on the poems:
    a. Memphis in Lower Egypt was the capital of the Old Kingdom; the great pyramids are across the Nile and extend for 20 miles to Gizeh.
    b. Babylon, held for centuries by the Assyrians, was famous for its Hanging Gardens, one of the ancient wonders of the world.
    c. Trivia's temple is the great Temple of Artemis (Diana) at Ephesus, an Ionian city near the western coast of Asia Minor.
    d. The famous altar of horns on Delos was supposed to have been constructed by Apollo from the horns of wild animals slain by his sister Artemis, goddess of the hunt.
    e. The Mausoleum was the tomb of Mausolus, king of Caria, and was constructed by his wife Artemisia.
    f. The Colossus (second poem) was the huge statue of Nero that originally stood in the vestibule of the **Domus Aurea.** It was 115 feet or 35 meters tall. Vespasian turned it into a statue of the Sun with rays surrounding its head.
    g. The scaffolds may have been for construction of the new buildings or for use in the shows.
    h. The "palace of a savage king" and the "proud domain" refer, of course, to Nero's **Domus Aurea,** which contained an elaborate park and

a lake and became the site of the Flavian Amphitheater.

i. The baths were the newly constructed Baths of Titus (*Rome and Environs*, p. 145, and *Pictorial Dictionary of Ancient Rome*, Vol. II, pp. 469–471), dedicated along with the Amphitheater.

j. The Claudian Colonnade was the colonnaded Neronian avenue 350 feet or 106 meters wide, built on the old Sacra Via and stretching from the Regia eastward to the **Domus Aurea**.

k. A simpler version of the third poem given here was included in the second student's book (page 72). In the present version, the geographical references of the original are retained and explained in the notes that follow.

l. Caesar, addressed in all three of the poems, is the Emperor Titus.

m. Rhodope and Haemus were mountains in Thrace, home of Orpheus.

n. The Sarmatians were a nomadic people north of the Black Sea.

o. Tethys was a goddess of the sea, wife of Oceanus: here by metonomy = the ocean.

p. The Sabaeans were a people of southwest Arabia.

q. The Cilicians in southeast Asia Minor were famous for their saffron perfume, with which the arena was sprinkled to cover the odor of beasts and blood.

r. The Sygambrians were a German tribe east of the Lower Danube.

Language Activity Book

1. Activity 45b: In order to emphasize the distinctions between the tenses, the teacher might ask students to give translations orally or in writing of the sentences with their various alternatives in this Activity.

2. Activity 45c: The following is a sample translation of the paragraph:

Cōnstat Vespasiānum et Titum amphitheātrum et thermās in locō Domūs Aureae aedificāvisse. Dīcunt populum Rōmānum thermās calidās admīrārī et multōs hominēs ab omnī parte imperiī ad lūdōs in amphitheātrō ventūrōs esse. "Titus," inquiunt, "Rōmam sibi reddidit."

CHAPTER 46: A DAY AT THE COLOSSEUM

Student's Book

1. **Background for "A Day at the Colosseum":**
   a. *Daily Life in Ancient Rome*, "The Amphitheatre," pp. 231–244; *Roman Life*, "Amphitheaters and Gladiators," pp. 282–303 (lavishly illustrated). Carcopino's and Johnston's chapters provide essential background; see

also *The Colosseum*, pp. 45–48, for a typical day at the amphitheater.

b. Seneca, *Epistulae Morales* VII, for a moralist's revulsion over the games (especially the combats of the **merīdiānī**) and their power to corrupt the spectators. Students might be directed to read the English translation of the extract from this letter on page 66 of the student's book during preliminary discussion of gladiatorial combats prior to reading the Latin story in Chapter 46. See also *Rome: Its People, Life and Customs*, pp. 252–254, for a negative evaluation of the sport in the amphitheater and its effects on the Romans. The passages from St. Augustine and Seneca in the cultural background readings at the end of this handbook (pp. 49–50) may also be read now or in conjunction with "Opposition to the Games" on page 66 of the student's book.

c. For the **tesserae** and seating in the Amphitheater, see *Daily Life in Ancient Rome*, pp. 234–236.

d. The term **pulvīnar** was originally applied to the cushioned couch on which images of the gods were placed at the festival and banquet called the **lectisternium** or "Spreading of the Bed." The term was later applied to any seat of honor such as that of the magistrate presiding over the races in the Circus or the displays in the Amphitheater.

e. The greeting, **Avē, Caesar! Moritūrī tē salūtant,** is preserved in Suetonius, *Claudius* XXI.

f. For the cries of the spectators, see the letter of Seneca referred to above and *Roman Voices*, p. 55, and below, note 10a.

2. In this chapter for the first time the accusative and infinitive in indirect statements are used after main verbs in the *past tense*:

. . . subitō vīdit Titum iam cōnsēdisse. (7–8)
. . . sciēbat Titum sērō ē lectō surgere solēre. (8–9)
Cui respondit Titus sē discēdere nōlle; sē nōndum satis vīdisse; merīdiānōs mox in arēnam ventūrōs esse. (27–28)

The use of the hinge word "that" should help students find the correct tense in English. If students have any difficulties in understanding the tense conversion, teachers might find it useful to provide English sentences in which students are asked to convert present to past and vice versa, e.g.:
   a. "The slave works today."
      He says the slave works today.
      He said the slave worked today.
   b. "The slave worked yesterday."
      He says the slave worked yesterday.
      He said the slave had worked yesterday.

Then, corresponding groups of sentences could be produced in Latin to show that a change from present to past tense in the main verb does not affect the tense of the infinitive in Latin but that it does affect the English translation:

    a. "Servus hodiē labōrat."
        Dīcit servum hodiē labōrāre.
        Dīxit servum hodiē labōrāre.

When the main verb is changed to a past tense, Latin retains the same tense in the infinitive as in the original statement; English changes to the past.

    b. "Servus heri labōrāvit."
        Dīcit servum heri labōrāvisse.
        Dīxit servum heri labōrāvisse.

Again, when the main verb is changed to a past tense, Latin retains the same tense in the infinitive as in the original statement; English changes to the pluperfect tense.

Further practice can be provided by turning the main verbs in Exercise 45b into the past tense and having students translate the sentences. Note that the future infinitive will then be translated in English with "would."

3. Words to be deduced: **fēmina** (2), **magistrātus** (5), **reservātus** (6), **circumspicere** (7), and **gladiātor** (18).

4. Invite students to identify the subjunctives and the types of clauses in which they are used in lines 5, 8, and 11.

5. Structures:

    a. Omission of the verb (2–3): this common Latin structure will be used with increasing frequency in the rest of the course. Compare **Mox tubicinēs et cornicinēs** (18).

    b. Anaphora: **Undique . . . ; undique. . . .** (2)

    c. Intruding genitive: **extrā amphitheātrī portās** (3)

    d. Interrupted sentence: **Cornēlius, cum . . . .** (5)

    e. Participial phrase: **ad locum magistrātibus reservātum** (5–6)

    f. Condensed sentence: **. . . respondit Titus sē . . . nōlle; sē . . . vīdisse; merīdiānōs . . . ventūrōs esse.** (27–28) To help students understand this sentence they should be encouraged to repeat **respondit Titus** before each accusative and infinitive.

6. Vocabulary and Grammar:

    a. **cōnsēdisse** (8): This verb, **cōnsīdō, cōnsīdere** (3), **cōnsēdī, cōnsessum,** means "to sit down," "to take one's seat." Contrast **sedeō, sedēre** (2), **sēdī, sessum,** which has the quite different meaning "to sit," "be sitting."

    b. Note the new meaning of **conicere** (10–11), previously used in the meaning "to throw."

    c. Students might be asked to explain why the ablative **amphitheātrō** (11) has no preposition, whereas English tends to say "in the amphitheater."

    d. **Caesar** (13) and **prīncipem** (15): See above, Chapter 45, Student's Book, note 8a. It is entirely appropriate that the voiced reference to the Emperor was **Caesar** since that was the title the Emperor preferred to hear.

    e. **amor ac dēliciae generis hūmānī** (13–14): This popular way of referring to Titus is quoted by Suetonius, *Titus* I. See the second teacher's handbook, Chapter 24, Student's Book, note 5f.

    f. **cōnstiterant** (17): This verb, **cōnsistō, cōnsistere** (3), **cōnstitī, cōnstitum,** means "to halt," "to stop," or "to stand still." The word **cōnstiterant** could accordingly be translated either "they had taken up their position" or "they were standing." Compare the note on **cōnsēdisse** above.

    g. **pugnābātur** (23): Treat this impersonal passive as a vocabulary item. Since the impersonal passive is a very difficult construction to understand, we propose to introduce several examples before attempting an explanation. It is hoped that students may be able to deduce **clāmābātur** (23), especially since it occurs so soon after **pugnābātur.** If they are unable to do so, simply give a translation rather than attempting a grammatical explanation.

    h. **nōbīs redeundum est** (24): Treat as a vocabulary item. Cf. **est cōnficienda** (45:27) and see above, Chapter 45, Student's Book, note 6.

7. Lines 26–29 are suitable for dictation, containing present, perfect, and future infinitives in indirect statements.

8. *Accusative and Infinitive (Indirect Statement) III:* After discussing this note with the students, the teacher should summarize the uses of the three different tenses of the infinitive in indirect statements, giving examples of direct statements using verbs in the present, future, imperfect, and perfect tenses and showing how they would be reported indirectly after main verbs first in the present tense and then in the perfect tense. The English translations should be carefully noted.

In order to simplify, students may be given two rules:

    a. The infinitive in the indirect statement is in the same tense as the verb in the corresponding direct statement, except that an imperfect tense in a direct statement is represented by a perfect infinitive when it is reported indirectly.

    b. The present infinitive describes an action going on at the same time as the action of the main verb; a perfect infinitive describes an action that happened or was going on prior to the action of the main verb; and a future infinitive describes an action that will take place after that of the main verb.

9. The sentences in Exercise 46b should be used to test and consolidate the students' understanding of the principles presented in the note *Accusative and Infinitive (Indirect Statement) III* and of the rules presented in 8a and b above. It is always useful to ask the students what the direct statement was that is here being presented indirectly. They may give the direct statement in either English or Latin. Then for each example the transformation of the direct to the indirect statement should be analyzed and the correct translation into English established.

10. *Gladiators:* For background reading, see note 1 above, and see Michael Grant, *Gladiators* (New York, Delacorte Press, 1968; no longer in print) and Howard Fast's popular novel, *Spartacus,* and the movie based on it.

   a. The oath **ūrī, vincīrī, verberārī, ferrōque necārī** is preserved in Petronius, *Satyricon* 117 and Seneca, *Epistulae Morales* 37. See *Roman Voices,* p. 54.
   b. Other inscriptions related to the gladiatorial contests will be found on page 57 of the student's book and in *Roman Voices,* "Amphitheater and Racetrack," pp. 43–68, and *Teacher's Guide to Roman Voices,* pp. 12–18.
   c. "a turn of the thumb": There is some controversy over the meaning of this phrase. Michael Grant (*Gladiators,* see above) says, "According to one familiar tradition, *thumbs up* meant that the man should be spared, *thumbs down* that he should not, and a relief seems to show the former gesture indicating mercy. The Latin terms, however (**vertere, premere pollicem**), might seem to suggest the contrary conclusion, the upward gesture imitating the fatal weapon and the downward one directing that the weapon should be thrown down."
   d. The riot in Pompeii described by Tacitus took place in A.D. 59.

11. Excercise 46c provides review of the accusative and infinitive in indirect statements depending on main verbs in both present and past tenses. Also, for the first time, passive infinitives are used in the indirect statements: **ductum esse** (7), **salūtārī** (8–9), **vulnerārī** (11), and **occīdī** (11). The perfect passive infinitive introduced here for the first time will be discussed in the note on page 55.

   Cum with the subjunctive meaning "when" is used twice (2 and 6–7) and once meaning "since" (14). In line 3, **mīlia** is to be deduced from **mīlle,** with which the students are familiar. Care should be taken with the perfect participles of deponent verbs: **regressus** (1) and **ingressī** (3).

   Pursuing the philosophy of the course, we have tried to stretch the minds of the students a little by using **clāmātum est** (8) and **redeundum erat** (13), hoping that they will be able to understand these on the basis of having had **clāmābātur** and **redeundum est** in the main story. If students find these phrases difficult, give them the meanings.

   Treat the potential subjunctive **crēdidissem** (4) as a vocabulary item and do not try to explain it at this stage (see Syntax, p. 45, of this handbook).

12. *Accusative and Infinitive (Indirect Statement) IV:* The perfect passive infinitive is formally introduced here. The Romans frequently omitted **esse** from the perfect passive and the future active infinitive forms.

13. *VERBS: Infinitives:* Examples of 3rd conjugation *-iō* verbs are not included in the tabulation of infinitives because they are formed in the same way as the infinitives of regular 3rd conjugation verbs.

14. The graffiti and inscriptions given at the end of the chapter come from *Roman Voices,* "Amphitheater and Racetrack," pp. 43–68, and *Teacher's Guide to Roman Voices,* pp. 12–18. They are numbers 9, 18, 22, and 39. The first one is an announcement written by a man named Aemilius Celer, unassisted, by moonlight, as he himself informs us in writing alongside the graffito itself; the second one is from a house on Nola Street in Pompeii; the third was written on a curse-tablet made of lead (*c.* A.D. 200) found in the amphitheater at Carthage; the fourth is from the tomb of a **rētiārius** at Parma.

   The **flāmen** of the first graffito was a priest of the living Emperor, Nero.

   With the curse-tablet (the third graffito), compare the curses against charioteers and their horses given in Chapter 26 of the second student's book and on page 44 in the cultural background readings at the end of the second teacher's handbook. See also the second teacher's handbook, Chapter 26, Student's Book, note 13.

15. *Other Shows in the Arena:* In addition to the passages quoted in the student's book on pages 58 and 59, there is a passage in the cultural background readings later in this handbook (pp. 48–49) from the account in the *Historia Augusta* of the Emperor Probus' triumphal celebrations in A.D. 281 that included extravagant slaughter of wild beasts.

Language Activity Book

1. Activity 46d gives practice with a variety of constructions used so far in the fourth student's book. In each pair of sentences, the construction in the sentence to translate from Latin to English serves as a model for the construction in the sentence to be translated from English to Latin.

2. In connection with word-family exercises such as Activity 46e, students should be reminded of how they can apply the skills in deducing words that they have been developing throughout their reading of the stories in the student's book.

CHAPTER 47: ANDROCLES AND THE LION

Student's Book

1. The reading passage in this chapter is freely adapted from Aulus Gellius, *Noctes Atticae* V.14. Gellius was a Roman writer of the 2nd century A.D. (*c.*

A.D. 130–c. A.D. 180). While studying in Athens he spent winter nights collecting material that he would later incorporate into his *Noctes Atticae,* originally 20 books of short chapters dealing with a wide variety of miscellaneous topics such as literature, history, religion, ritual, and philosophy. The work is full of fascinating stories and cultural information about the Romans.

The language activity book contains extracts of Gellius' original Latin version of the story for students to translate. Teachers may also have their students read the two-act play, *Androcles and the Lion,* by George Bernard Shaw (1856–1950), the great Irish dramatist of ideas. Shaw makes Androcles a convert to Christianity and turns the story into an amusing satire of the Christian religion. As with the Ovidian and Shakespearean versions of the story of Pyramus and Thisbe, contrasts may here be drawn between the narrative version of the story in the ancient author and the dramatic version in the modern, and there are opportunities for essays and creative writing.

2. No major new points of grammar are introduced in this chapter.

3. The reading passage is particularly useful for directing the attention of students to some of the subtleties of tense usage. For example, the distinction between perfect and imperfect is drawn several times, particularly in the first paragraph: **dabātur** "was being given" (1); the gasp of admiration produced by **fuērunt** in line 2 followed by the more leisurely survey of the lions suggested by **vidēbātur** (2). The perfect **stetit** (5) depicts the suddenness of the action, while **appropinquābat** later in the same sentence (5) is best translated "began to approach." **Spectāvit** (8) suggests the act of opening the eyes, while **stābant** (8) conveys the impression of peaceful inactivity, whereas one might have expected active violence in this situation.

4. Note the uses of the present participle: **admīrāns** (5), **movēns** (6), **gemēns et dolēns** (15), **petēns** (18), and **vescentēs** (21). All of these are used in sentences where the main verb is in a past tense and will have to be translated to show that the action of the participle was going on at the same time as that of the main verb in past time.

5. Words to be deduced: **bēstiārius** (1), **introdūcere** (3), **prope** (6: adverb, "nearly"), **mīrābilis** (12), **condemnāre** (22), and **līberāre** (24).

6. Structures:
   a. Word order:
   Omnēs spectātōribus admīrātiōnī fuērunt leōnēs. . . . (1–2)
   . . . laetī ibi . . . et homō et leō. (8–9)
   Androclem . . . rogāvit Caesar. . . . (10–11)
   . . . datusque eī leō. (24)
   b. Linking **quī** and postponement of the subordinating conjunction: **Quem cum. . . .** (4)

7. Treat **admīrātiōnī fuērunt** (2) as a vocabulary item. Further examples of the predicative dative or dative of purpose and examples of the double dative construction will be met in the following chapters and in the fifth student's book.

8. Ad pugnam (3): Although students will have no difficulty in translating this phrase, the opportunity might be taken to show that **ad** conveys the notion of *purpose*: "He had been brought in *for the purpose of* a fight." Compare the similar phrase **ad bēstiās** (22), which suggests that the magistrate, when condemning Androcles, was thinking of the use to which he might put him, i.e., to provide entertainment at the games.

9. Attention should be paid to the ablative absolutes (7, 8, 19, and 23). The vocabulary list gives a translation of **mūtuā recognitiōne factā** (8), but students should be able to see how each word contributes to the meaning of the clause.

10. attentius (7–8) provides practice in translating the comparative adverb.

11. Students may be asked to locate and identify the three clauses using verbs in the subjunctive (4, 11, and 16).

12. Vocabulary and minor grammatical notes:
   a. Students may be interested to know that **mānsuētus** (17) comes from **manus** "hand" and **suēscō, suēscere** (3), "to become accustomed to."
   b. Special attention should be called to the fact that **parcere** (11) takes the dative case and **vescī** (21) the ablative. Note the irregular dative **sōlī** (11); cf. **utrīque** (43:7) and **alterī** (43:9). Note **multō** (14), ablative of degree of difference, and note **ūnō pede** (15), ablative of respect.

13. *Building Up the Meaning VII:* Teachers should constantly encourage students to work their way through each sentence, tackling the words, phrases, and clauses in the order in which they occur, thus building up the meaning of the sentence as the clues unfold. This technique of anticipating what is likely to follow certain clues will become increasingly important as students are introduced to more and more major items of syntax and to more complex sentences.

14. Exercises 47a and b: Students should be asked to identify each subordinate clause in these sentences (e.g., indirect statement, indirect question) and to identify and explain the tense of the verb used in each subordinate clause. In Exercise 47a, No. 4, a present subjunctive **(lambat)** appears in the indirect question (the present subjunctive will be formally introduced in Chapter 49).

15. Versiculī: "Another Example of Caesar's Leniency," page 120: To be deduced: **palma** (9).

Language Activity Book

1. Activity 47a is similar to Activity 43a and gives

students a chance to read and think about a substantial story, part of it in English and part in Latin. The teacher should be ready to give help with translation of the Latin as needed.

While the version of the story in the student's book uses the more familiar (Greek) spelling of the name Androcles, the text of Gellius gives the Latin form, Androclus. Gaius Caesar, who presides at this beast-fight in the Circus Maximus and is otherwise known as Caligula, reigned from A.D. 37 to A.D. 41.

The following are sample translations of the passages from Gellius:

> "In the Circus Maximus," he said, "the people were given a very impressive wild-beast fight. I myself saw it, since I happened to be at Rome," he said. "There were many raging wild animals, surpassing beasts in size, and of each of them either the appearance or the ferocity was unusual. But beyond all the others," he said, "the huge size of the lions was a matter for wonder, and of one beyond all the others."

> "The slave of a man of consular rank was brought in among several others assigned to fight the wild beasts; the slave's name was Androclus. When that lion saw him from afar, suddenly," he said, "as if in wondrous admiration he stood still and then gradually and quietly, as if recognizing (him), he approached the man."

> "Then you could see the man and the lion, as if with mutual recognition, happy," he said, "and congratulating (one another)."

> "Then," he said, "when the midday sun was fierce and scorching I found a certain remote cave that offered a hiding place, and I entered and hid in it. And not long after, this lion came to the same cave, with one foot lame and bloody, giving forth groans and sighs, (with which he was) seeking pity for the pain and torture of his wound."

> "Then and there," he said, "I pulled out a huge thorn clinging to the bottom of his foot, and I pressed out the pus that had formed in the innermost part of the wound, and I very carefully and now without great fear dried (the wound) thoroughly and wiped away the blood." Relieved by that effort and treatment of mine, the lion then lay down with his foot placed in my hands and rested; from that day the lion and I lived for three whole years in the same cave and with the same food."

> "Afterwards," he said, "we saw Androclus and the lion tied with a thin thong going from shop to shop in the whole city; Androclus was given money, the lion was sprinkled with flowers, and all who met them everywhere were saying, 'This lion is the man's guest, and this man is the lion's doctor.'"

2. The following are hints of possible answers to the questions in Activity 47b:
   1. Some readers will feel that Gellius' introductory paragraph does not instill confidence in Apion's credibility as a storyteller. Students will differ as to how credible they think his actual story is.
   2. Students might note Androclus' mention of the cruelty of his master and the fact that he was desperate enough to welcome death.
   3. Students might mention the lion's groaning to gain sympathy for his plight, his gentle lifting of his paw to appeal for help, his generosity in bringing food to Androclus, and, of course, his expression of gratitude in the Circus Maximus.
   4. Students might point out that the lion and Androclus recognize each other's plight and that they care for one another attentively and sympathetically (Androclus' healing of the lion's wound being matched by the lion's generosity in giving the best parts of his quarry to Androclus).
   5. His master apparently condemns him to death simply because he was a runaway.
   6. The answer to this question would include the notions of generosity and of sympathy for the plight of another living creature.
   7. Answers will vary but might include the idea that generosity is rewarded.

CHAPTER 48: AUDIENCE REACTION

Student's Book

1. a. The initial dialogue provides a spectator's view of the story told in the previous Chapter.
   b. No new grammar is formally discussed in this chapter, but a number of present and perfect subjunctives are introduced in indirect questions. There is intensive practice with indirect statement.

2. Word to be deduced: **tigris** (4)

3. Most of the indirect statements in the first scene follow main verbs in the present tense (8, 9, 10, 14, 14−15, 17−18, and 20), while one indirect statement in the first scene (4−6) and all in the second scene (23, 28−29, 30−31, and 31−32) follow main verbs in a past tense. Infinitives of all tenses, active and passive, are used. All of this provides excellent material for review of accurate translation of Latin indirect statements into good English.

4. The verb **vidēre** may be followed by an indirect statement using the accusative and infinitive (8, 10, and 20) or by a noun (or pronoun) and a participle, both in the accusative case, e.g., 16, 17, 19, 25−26, and 33−34. The latter construction is particularly used when it is a matter of seeing something or someone *in a particular state*. Compare the constructions with **audiō** described in the note on page 62 of the student's book.

5. The passage contains a number of indirect questions. Some (21, 29–30, and 32) depend on verbs in a past tense and use the familiar pluperfect subjunctive. Others introduce a new feature of grammar in that they depend on verbs in the present tense and use either the present (3, 4, 18, and 20) or the perfect (13 and 27) subjunctive. (For an earlier occurrence of an indirect question with the present subjunctive, see 45:10.) Students will have little or no trouble with the new present and perfect subjunctive forms, which will be introduced formally in Chapter 49. Some attention should be called to them at this stage, but a full discussion of sequence of tenses should be saved for Chapter 49.

6. redeāmus (33): Again, as in 42:6, the hortatory subjunctive should be treated as a vocabulary item, with formal discussion delayed until the fifth student's book.

7. Lines 28–32 are suitable for dictation, being descriptive in nature and showing a variety of subordinate constructions.

8. Versiculī: "Androcles' True Bravery," page 121 In line 4, the delay of the antecedent (**manum**) of **quā** (abl. with **vescī**) may prove difficult. Be sure students remember that **manus** is feminine. Lines 5 and 6 may also prove difficult: "I guess, Caesar, that the foolish folk (i.e., the spectators) have thoughts such as this (i.e., the thoughts expressed in lines 1–4), while you are sparing both the dinner and at the same time the wild beast." **Cēnae** and **ferae** are datives with **parcente,** and may be interpreted as hendiadys (a single idea expressed through two nouns): "the wild beast's dinner," i.e., Androcles. In line 7, **audācia** is to be deduced.

9. *Gladiatorial Fever:* Throughout *Satire* VIII, Juvenal criticizes the decadence of some of the nobility of his day. In this extract he makes the point to a young nobleman that, despite the apparent glamour of the arena, the gladiator's lot is no life for a young man of noble birth. The Gracchus in the passage has sunk about as low as he possibly can in that the **rētiāriī** were despised by the other gladiators and were given the poorest quarters in the school. He does not even have the decency to conceal his identity by wearing a helmet. Compare the following description of the Emperor Commodus (sole Emperor A.D. 180–192):

> At gladiatorial shows he would come to watch and stay to fight, covering his bare shoulders with a purple cloth. And it was his custom, moreover, to order the insertion in the city-gazette of everything he did that was base or foul or cruel, or typical of a gladiator. . . . He entitled the Roman people the "People of Commodus," since he had very often fought as a gladiator in their presence. And although the people regularly applauded him in his frequent combats as though he were a god, he became convinced that he was being

> laughed at, and gave orders that the Roman people should be slain in the Amphitheater by the marines who spread the awnings.
> *Historia Augusta; Commodus* XV
> —tr. David Magie

The passage from Seneca's *Epistles* is included to give some idea of the cruelty of the games. Both passages show that not all Romans were interested in the games and that some were clearly disgusted by them. St. Augustine in a famous passage in his *Confessions* (see the cultural background readings at the end of this handbook, pp. 49–50) describes the overwhelming psychological impact of the bloodthirsty violence of the games even on a person who tried to hold out against the temptation. Seneca also recognized the detrimental effect of the games on the character of the spectators (see the passage on page 50 of the cultural background readings).

Language Activity Book

Along with the reading from Cicero, students may be directed to the passage from Pliny's *Natural History* in the cultural background readings at the end of this handbook and in particular the description of Pompey's elephants (page 49) and the compassion they evoked among the spectators.

In addition to the questions at the end of Activity 48a, the last of which could provide the topic for a formal essay, the teacher may assign other topics for written work based on the Latin stories about the Amphitheater in the student's book, the readings from ancient authors in Chapters 44 to 48, and the cultural background readings at the end of the teacher's handbook. Topics for written work might focus on the reasons for the Romans' love of violence and bloodshed in the arena and its impact on Roman character or on comparisons with modern life, violent spectator sports (e.g., bull fighting), and addictive, graphic violence in the movies and on television. There is abundant opportunity here for exploration of the similarities and the differences between Roman and modern societies. Another possibility is for a student to pretend to be a Roman citizen who is tired of the atrocities in the arena and to prepare a written speech to try to persuade the senate, the Emperor, and the Roman people that the time has come to put an end to this violence.

WORD STUDY XII

1. The aims of this section are:
  a. to explain the formation of Latin nouns using the suffixes **-ārium/-ōrium, -ūra,** and **-mentum**
  b. to explain how English derivatives are formed from Latin words with these suffixes.

2. In support of the discussion of the noun suffix **-ārium,** some review of the adjectival and substantive uses of the suffix **-ārius** would be helpful (see Word

Study V), e.g., **librārius, -a, -um**, *pertaining to books;* **librārius, -ī** *(m), bookseller.*

3. Teachers should make some mention of the adjectival use of the suffix **-ōrius**, a suffix very similar to but not as common as **-ārius**, e.g., **ambulātōrius, -a, -um**, *movable* or *suitable for walking* (derivative: *ambulatory*). The suffix **-ory** is very common in English, although many of these words have no classical Latin counterparts, e.g., *preparatory, contradictory, satisfactory.*

4. In Exercise 1, **avis, sōl,** and **tabula** have not yet been seen, but will be introduced in later chapters. The capitalization of **Tabulārium** indicates specifically the building in the Roman Forum, referred to in Chapter 50. In connection with **caldārium**, students should be reminded of **tepidārium** and **frīgidārium,** and their formation should be discussed (i.e., from **tepidus** and **frīgidus**). Students should be encouraged to give English derivatives of the Latin nouns in Exercise 1, whenever they exist, e.g., *respository, aviary. Solarium* is unchanged in English, and the English derivative of **armārium** is a borrowing from French: *armoire.*

5. In Exercise 2, students must follow the directions carefully in order to produce the Latin source of the base of the English word, rather than the Latin noun ending in **-ārium/-ōrium**; e.g., the source of the base of *infirmary* is **īnfirmus**; the more proximate source, "**īnfirmārium**," is not found in classical Latin. In fact, the only word in Exercise 2 for which there is a corresponding classical Latin noun ending in **-ārium/-ōrium** is *diary*, from the Latin noun **diārium**, *daily journal* (plural: **diāria**, *daily ration*), which is ultimately derived from **diēs**.

6. In Exercise 3, No. 5, students should have no difficulty producing the English derivative *posture* by dropping the **i** from the Latin **positūra**.

7. The noun suffix **-mentum** is closely related to the noun suffix **-men, -minis.** In fact, for many nouns ending in **-mentum,** there are corresponding nouns ending in **-men,** e.g., **augmentum** and **augmen, regimentum** and **regimen.**

8. In Exercise 5, No. 1, students will find that the English words *compliment* and *complement* are both ultimately derived from *complēre*. *Compliment* is spelled with an *i* because it comes into English through the Spanish word *cumplimiento,* from the verb *cumplir* (derived from **complēre**), meaning "to do what is proper or courteous"—hence the meaning of *compliment.*

In No. 3, students will be reminded of **pavimentum** (first seen in Chapter 42), but they should be careful to change the **i** to *e* in the English derivative *pavement.*

9. Exercise 6 illustrates the variety of spelling alterations in the stem of the original Latin verb, e.g., **sedē-** becomes *sedi-* in *sediment,* **monē-** becomes *monu-* in *monument,* and **augē-** drops the stem vowel in *augment.* The suffix *-ment* is very common in English. Students should be cautioned, however, that many

English words with the suffix *-ment* are purely English formations and have no source in classical Latin ending in **-mentum**, e.g., , *amazement, government,* and *enjoyment.*

10. *Inceptive Verbs:* Also called *inchoative* verbs (**incohō**, *to begin*), inceptives normally have no perfect or supine stems of their own, but use the perfect and supine stems of the simple verbs, e.g., the perfect of **conticēscō** is **conticuī** (cf. **tacuī**); and the perfect stem of **convalēscō is convaluī** (cf. **valuī**).

REVIEW XI

Student's Book

1. The main grammatical features in Chapters 44–48 that require review are:
  a. indirect statement with the main verb in present or a past tense and the infinitive in the present, future, or perfect tense, active or passive
  b. the use of **sē** in indirect statements
  c. forms of the infinitive
  d. the irregular verbs **fīō** and **mālō**

2. Exercise XIa provides review of indirect questions, ablative absolutes, and circumstantial clauses as well as of indirect statements. Students should become accustomed to identifying and labeling each of these subordinate constructions, to identifying the tense and voice of each infinitive, subjunctive, and participle, to stating the temporal relationship between the main and subordinate clauses, and to making their translations express this temporal relationship. This is a long exercise, and teachers may wish to do some of the sentences in class and assign others for homework.

3. Exercise XIb
  a. Words to be deduced: **tyrannus** (1), **magnificentia** (3), **odōrēs** (8; "incense"), **onerō** (8), **fortūnātus** (8), and **dēmittere** (11; to let down, suspend).
  b. Three new uses of the subjunctive are introduced in contexts that make them immediately intelligible:
  indirect command: **. . . ōrāvit tyrannum ut sibi abīre licēret. . . .** (13)
  causal clause in which the reason given is that of someone other than the author: **. . . quod iam beātus esse nōllet.** (13)
  relative clause of characteristic: **. . . cui semper aliquī terror impendeat.** (14–15)

4. The teacher may introduce the following **sententiae** in conjunction with the moral of the story in Exercise XIb:
Nihil est ab omnī parte beātum.
No one (literally, *nothing*) *is happy in every way.* (Horace, *Odes* II.16.27–28)

Contentum suīs rēbus esse maximae sunt certissimae-que dīvitiae.

To be content with one's own possessions is the greatest and most reliable form of riches. (Cicero, *Paradoxa Stoicorum* VI.51)

Tūta est hominum tenuitās. Magnae perīclō sunt opēs obnoxiae.

Slender means are safe for men. Great wealth is subject to danger. (Phaedrus, *Fables* II.7, 13—14)

Language Activity Book

1. Activity RXIa: In No. 8, students may need help with the phrase "groaning with fear," but the phrase **metū exanimātī** (47:6—7) has provided a model for the use of the ablative here.

The following are sample translations of the sentences in RXIa:
1. Dāmoclēs dīcit sē dēgustāre vītam Dionȳsiī cupere.
2. Dionȳsius putat hanc vītam Dāmoclēn nōn dēlectātūram esse.
3. Dionȳsius scit nūllum tyrannum umquam omnīnō beātum fuisse.
4. Putābat vītam tyrannī Dāmoclēn rē vērā territūram esse.
5. Sciēbat eam saepe sē terruisse.
6. Dionȳsius iubet Dāmoclēn pulchrīs vestibus induī, in lectō aureō recumbere et ā puerīs capillātīs dīligentissimē ministrārī.
7. Dionȳsius sciēbat gladium suprā caput virī beātī dēmissum esse.
8. Adstantēs audīvērunt Dāmoclēn metū gementem.
9. Omnēs cīvēs urbis audīvērunt cūr Dāmoclēs beātus esse nōllet.
10. Dāmoclēs mālēbat homō vulgāris iterum fierī.

CHAPTER 49: NOTHING EVER HAPPENS

Student's Book

1. a. This chapter introduces result clauses, possibly the easiest of the clauses introduced by **ut** because of the presence of the very strong clue words such as **tam** and **tantus**.
   b. The present and perfect forms of the subjunctive are tabulated.
   c. Now that students have been introduced to all four tenses of the subjunctive, we introduce the concept of sequence of tenses and illustrate it with examples of indirect questions (based on lines 6—7 of the story, the only occurrences of the perfect subjunctive in the story), in which the entire system of sequence of tenses may be demonstrated most easily. It should be noted, however, that result clauses often appear to violate the general rules for sequence of tenses.
   d. Three of the most common impersonal verbs are introduced: **taedet, oportet,** and **placet.**

   e. A contrast between nature's joyfulness and Cornelia's pensive mood signals a return from the public spectacles in the arena to the private life of the family. The plans of Cornelius and Aurelia for the marriage of their daughter are revealed and will be carried out in Chapter 52. Interwoven with the theme of Cornelia's marriage is that of Marcus' coming of age, and these joyful rites of passage from childhood to adulthood are balanced in the last chapter with a final rite of passage, Titus' death and burial.
   f. The present Chapter concludes with background material on Roman weddings, the betrothal ceremony of Valerius and Cornelia, and an unadapted Latin reading with English translation from Aulus Gellius.

2. Words and phrase to be deduced: **sōlitūdō** (3), **serva** (6), **nōbilis** (20), **in mātrimōnium dūcere** (21), and **perturbātus** (23). Note that **lūcēbat** (1) has a different meaning here ("was shining") from the meaning with which it was used earlier ("it was light," "it was day"; see 8:1).

3. Result clauses: There are three result clauses with the new present subjunctive forms (**ut . . . videam,** 4; **ut . . . loquātur,** 5; and **ut . . . faciant,** 6); the fourth result clause has a familiar imperfect subjunctive (**ut . . . posset,** 23). The teacher should emphasize the clue words in the main clauses that anticipate the result clauses: **tantum** (4), **tam** (4), and **adeō** (6 and 23). The endings of the present subjunctives should be noted and contrasted with the familiar indicative endings, but full presentation of the forms of the present subjunctive may be left until the charts on pages 75 and 76 are studied.

4. The three new impersonal verbs are given in phrases in the vocabulary and should be treated in the context of the sentences within which they occur in the text:
   "Mē taedet sōlitūdinis." (2—3)
   "Festīnāre tē oportet." (10—11)
   "'Nōn decet patrem . . . dēspondēre fīliam. . . .'" (18)
To these may be added the impersonal **placet,** introduced in Exercise 32e, line 3, and used three times in the present story (22, 24), e.g.:
   "Mihi quoque placet." (24)
The impersonal **licet** may also be added to the list; it occurred first in Chapter 19:
   "Licetne nōbīs," inquit Marcus, "hīc cēnāre?" (19:7)
Other examples may be given, such as the following:
   Dāvum taedet labōris.
   Puerōs taedet lūdōrum.
   Cornēliam oportet festīnāre.
   Cīvem Rōmānum oportet festīnāre.
   Patrem decet uxōrem cōnsulere.
   Prīnceps decet senātōrēs cōnsulere.
   Id quod Cornēlius dīxit Cornēliae placet.
   Valeriō Cornēliam in mātrimōnium dūcere licet.

Some students will want to know the exact meaning of the more idiomatic impersonal verbs:

Taedet is a transitive verb meaning "it makes" or "there is a making" someone (accusative case, direct object) "tired, weary, or sick" of something (genitive case, expressing cause). Thus, **Mē taedet sōlitūdinis** means "There is a making me sick of loneliness" or "I am sick of being alone."

There is a subtle distinction between **oportet** and **decet,** as is shown by the following translations as given in the *Oxford Latin Dictionary*:

oportet: "It is demanded by some principle or standard, it is proper, right, requisite. . . ."

decet = decōrum est: "It is becoming," i.e., in "accord with approved standards of taste or behavior . . . ." "It is right, proper, fitting. . . ."

Activity 49e in the language activity book gives practice in use of the impersonal verbs.

5. The double dative construction in line 13 **(id quod erat eī admīrātiōnī et cūrae)** is an expansion of the construction in 47:1−2.

6. The passage provides review of some of the uses of the ablative without a preposition: **caelō serēnō** (1), **trīstī vultū** (2), **gravī vultū** (14), **maximā īrā** (17−18), **īnsciā mātre** (18−19), and **submissā vōce** (23−24).

7. Structures:
It will be noted that some of the sentences which appear in this Chapter are longer and more complex than the students have been accustomed to so far in the course. It is therefore all the more important that they be encouraged to build up the meaning of each sentence as it unfolds, rather than hop about from one part to another looking for subject, object, and verb.
Condensed sentence:
Nōn intellegō cūr . . . neglēxerint, cūr . . . dīxerit. (6−7)
Word order:
. . . vīdit adesse et patrem et mātrem. . . . (12)
. . . ūnā cōnstituimus et ego et māter tua. . . . (19−20)

8. Vocabulary: Note that **observō** is pronounced *ops-*, as **urbs** is pronounced *urps*.

9. *VERBS: Subjunctive Mood II:* Emphasize how easy the forms of the present subjunctive are to recognize. While an *a* is characteristic of the 1st conjugation in the indicative, *e* is characteristic in the subjunctive. All of the other conjugations show an *a*. The active and passive personal endings are nearly the same as those used in the indicative. The forms of the perfect subjunctive are identical with those of the future perfect indicative, except for the 1st person singular.

10. *Sequence of Tenses:* The note and the examples cited should be thoroughly discussed and the principles and terminology involved thoroughly understood. Students will need to be informed at a later stage in their study of Latin that the perfect tense when used in the sense of a *present-perfect* follows the rules for *primary* sequence.

11. Exercise 49b provides intensive practice with result clauses. No. 6 is deliberately *not* a result clause. The clue word which gives least help is **tālis** (No. 7), and some additional help may be necessary.

12. *Roman Weddings I:* For further background information on marriage and weddings, see *Roman Family Life*, "Engagement, Marriage and Babies," pp. 17−25, and the accompanying *Aspects of Roman Life Folder A* (white card 5.10, "Husbands and Wives in a Roman Family," and yellow source cards 1.18, "The Rights of the Head of the Family," 1.19 "The Qualities of a Good Wife," and 1.23, "Love and Marriage"); *Rome: Its People, Life and Customs*, pp. 114−119; *Roman Life*, "Marriage Customs and Roman Women," pp. 126−139; and *Daily Life in Ancient Rome*, "Marriage, Woman, and the Family," pp. 76−100.

Students may be encouraged to compare engagements, bridal showers, prenuptial parties, wedding ceremonies, married life, and divorce in modern societies. The rites surrounding engagement, marriage, and divorce tell much about the status and position of women in society, and students may be invited to consider some of the larger aspects of roles and positions in life as they are determined and shaped by the respective society's marriage conventions. There are opportunities here for discussion and written work of various sorts.

13. Exercise 49c is an important one and should not be omitted. Besides picking up some of the points made in *Roman Weddings I* and providing continuity in the family story, it contains an example of an indirect command (**invītāverat ut prōnuba esset,** 4−5; cf. Review XI, Exercise XIb, line 13), a construction that will be dealt with in Chapter 50. Note the following points of style, vocabulary, and grammar:

a. The sentence **Deinde, silentiō factō. . . .** (8−9) provides useful practice in studying the importance of word order in deciding how to group words: **vultū dēmissō** should be taken with **ingressa,** and **in ātrium** with **dēducta est.** Note too how the sentence tells us accurately the order in which things occurred: first, there was silence; second, Cornelia appeared at the door; third, she was escorted from there into the room.

b. The word **contrā** (9) is used in the sense "facing" or "opposite" (cf. 46:16) rather than the more common usage "against."

c. In line 10, **uxōrem** "as my wife" is in apposition to **fīliam tuam** and so in the accusative case.

d. **"Spondeō"** (12): Although English would most naturally use an expression such as "I do" or "Yes," Latin idiom repeats the verb: **Spondēsne? Spondeō.**

e. **tertiō digitō:** See *The Ring Finger* on page 81 of the student's book.

Words to be deduced: **rescrībere** (3), **dēdūcere** (9), **spōnsus** (14), and **spōnsa** (14).

14. *The Ring Finger:* As we did with the Latin and English passages earlier in the fourth student's book and in the third student's book, we recommend that a student in class read aloud the English translation first and that another student then read the Latin. The Latin may then be translated clause by clause by students in succession. Activity 49f in the language activity book is an English to Latin exercise in which students translate a simpler version of this story into Latin. Students' attention should therefore be directed closely to the language and idiom of the Latin version of Gellius in the student's book.

The Greek words in the Latin and in the English translation may be transliterated into English as follows: *anatomas* (acc. pl.) and *anatomai* (nom. pl.). The word literally means "a cutting" (*tome*) "up" (*ana-*). Compare the English derivative *anatomy*.

Language Activity Book

1. Activities 49a and b provide practice with formation of the subjunctive in all tenses.

2. Activity 49c provides practice with sequence of tenses in indirect questions, while Activity 49d provides similar practice with result clauses.

3. The pairs of sentences in Activity 49e provide practice with the impersonal verbs.

4. Activity 49f is based on the story from Gellius in the student's book. The following is a sample translation of the paragraph:

Veterēs Graecī ānulum in digitō sinistrae manūs quī minimō est proximus habuērunt. Rōmānī quoque ānulīs sīc plērumque ūsitātī sunt. Ōlim in Aegyptō virī nervum tenuissimum ab eō digitō ad cor pergentem repperērunt. Proptereā nōn īnscītum vīsum est ānulō in eō digitō ūsitārī, quī conēxus esse cum corde vidēbātur.

5. Students should be encouraged to use an English dictionary in doing Activity 49g. This will help with questions such as the third part of No.6.

CHAPTER 50: MARCUS COMES OF AGE

Student's Book

1. For coming of age ceremonies, see *Roman Life*, pp. 146–147.

The **Līberālia** celebrated on 17 March was the festival of Liber, the Italian god of wine and fertility, who was associated with the Greek Dionysus or Bacchus. It was essentially a rustic, country festival concerned with healthy growth of the vineyards. Vergil describes the country festival as follows (*Georgics* II.385–396, translation adapted from that of H. R. Fairclough):

In this way Italian farmers, a breed of men sent from Troy, sport with rude verses and unre-

strained laughter and put on hideous masks of hollow cork. They call on you, O Bacchus, in joyful songs, and for you they hang from the tall pines little faces that wave in the breezes. It is for this reason that every vineyard ripens with generous growth; fullness comes to hollow valleys and deep glades and to every spot to which the god has turned his handsome face. Rightly, then, in our country-songs we will sing for Bacchus the praise he claims, bringing him cakes and dishes. The doomed he-goat, led by its horn, will stand at the altar, and we will roast its rich flesh on spits of hazel wood.

The purpose of the masks may have been to frighten away evil spirits.

Ovid could think of a number of possible reasons why the **Līberālia** was a favored occasion for boys to assume the **toga virīlis** or the **toga lībera** as he calls it (*Fasti* III.771–788, translation adapted from that of Sir J. G. Frazer):

It remains for me to discover why the gown of liberty is given to boys, fair Bacchus, on your day, whether it is because you seem to be always a boy and a youth, and your age is midway between the two; or it may be that, because you are a father, fathers commend to your care and divine keeping their sons to whom they guarantee their love; or it may be that because you are Liber, the gown of liberty is assumed and a freer life is entered upon under your auspices. Or was it because, in the days when the ancients tilled the fields more diligently and a senator labored on his ancestral land, when a consul exchanged the bent plough for the rods and axes of office, and it was no crime to have calloused hands, the country folk used to come into the city for the games . . . and the day therefore seemed suitable for conferring the gown, so that a crowd might gather around the young man?

One possibility Ovid does not mention is that the **Līberālia** was the favored day for children to assume the **toga virīlis** simply because of a play on the words **Līberālia** and **līberī**, "children."

2. The reading passage is slightly longer than usual. Indirect command is the main new syntactical feature of the chapter. The story contains nine examples (4–5, 10, 10–11, 13, 13–14, 15–16, 25, 29, and 35), which have been written to allow **ut** to be translated by the English infinitive. The one example of **nē** ("not to," 13) is given in the vocabulary. All examples are in secondary sequence with verbs in the imperfect subjunctive.

The subordinate clauses commonly described as *indirect commands* may be introduced by verbs of ordering or requesting (e.g., in the story: **invītāverat**, 4; **rogābat**, 10; **praecipiēbat**, 10; **ōrābant**, 13; and **imperābat**, 14). We therefore title the grammar note on this construction *Telling to, Asking to: Indirect Commands*.

3. Words to be deduced: **sēdecim** (3), **familia** (15), **puerīlis** (23), and **pūblicus** (31).

4. Structures:
   a. Anaphora:
      Omnēs sciēbant . . .; omnēs. . . . (5)
      Aderant . . .; aderant . . .; aderant . . .; aderant. . . . (16–17)
      Cūnctī . . .; cūnctī. . . . (17–18)
   b. List: **. . . tumultūs, strepitūs, clāmōris.** (7)
   c. Linking **quī**:
      Quō factō. . . . (25)
      Quō cum. . . . (28)
      Quibus rēbus cōnfectīs. . . . (32)
   d. Word order: **. . . est dēductus.** (27)
   e. Interrupted phrase: **. . . propter tantam ergā sē benevolentiam. . . .** (33–34)

5. Minor notes on vocabulary and grammar:
   a. **ab iānuā prōgressus, in ipsō līmine . . . stāret** (8–9): The **iānua** is the double door in the entrance passage some way off the street; **līmen** refers to the actual threshold of the passageway.
   b. **rogābat quis esset et quid vellet** (9–10): See Exercise 50c. After study of the indirect commands in this reading passage, this example of indirect questions should be noted by way of contrast. Stress the distinction between "asking something" (indirect question) and "asking *someone to do* something" (indirect command).
   c. **Hī . . . ōrābant nē sē dīmitteret; ille . . . eīs. . . .** (13): The difference between the third person pronouns **sē** and **eīs** is very clearly illustrated here. Compare also **in sē conversōs esse** (21), **ergā sē** (34), and **apud sē** (35). In addition, **hī** and **ille** are well contrasted in line 13.
   d. At some point in study of the passage, students should be asked to locate all examples of ablative absolutes and translate them (15, 25, 27, 28, 32).
   e. **familiam** (15): The attention of students should be drawn to the use of this term to denote the entire household, including the slaves. Compare **Laribus familiāribus** (23).
   f. **plūrimī clientium** (16–17): Note the partitive genitive with **plūrimī** and the i-stem noun.
   g. **omnēs** and **cūnctī** (17–18): The word **omnēs** denotes the total number or total amount, whereas **cūnctī** expresses the idea of corporate feeling or action. For example, in this sentence, **omnēs** suggests that the slaves and freedmen were *all* there, not a single individual being absent; **cūnctī** tells us that all who were present behaved *as a united body* in their expressions of gladness.
   h. **togam praetextam atque bullam . . . dēpositās** (22–23): Students may need a little help with the plural agreement (**dēpositās**) following the two singular nouns **togam** and **bullam**.

   i. **multīs comitantibus** (27): This is a useful example of an ablative absolute in the present tense denoting that the crowd was following at the same time as Marcus was being taken to the Forum. See also **ēgressum** (32), showing that the shouting started *after* Marcus came out, whereas **ēgredientem** would have indicated that it happened *as he was coming out*.

6. Lines 32–35 are suitable for dictation.

7. Exercises 50a and b give practice with indirect commands. Teachers may wish to postpone them until after discussion of the note on page 85.

8. *Telling to, Asking to: Indirect Commands:* Teachers should explicitly call to students' attention the contrast in the examples at the beginning of this note between the Latin that expresses indirect commands with **ut** and the subjunctive and English that uses a simple infinitive. When translating from English to Latin it will be especially important for students to remember not to use the infinitive in translating purpose clauses.

   Hortor appears here for the first time; note that **obsecrō** is pronounced *ops-*, with the accent on the first syllable.

9. Exercise 50c: See note 5b above. In teaching the concept of indirect commands, it is important that students realize that behind each indirect command there is a direct command ("telling to") or request ("asking to"), just as behind each indirect question there is a direct question and behind each indirect statement there is a direct statement. In Exercise 50c, Nos. 2 and 3, students are asked to formulate the implied direct commands, requests, or questions in English. In Activity 50a in the language activity book, students will be asked to produce in Latin the direct commands or requests that lie behind the indirect commands or requests in the story at the beginning of the chapter.

10. Exercise 50d: In Nos. 1, 4, 6, and 10, indirect commands in primary sequence with verbs in the present subjunctive occur for the first time in the readings or exercises. The concept of sequence of tenses should be reviewed, and the sentences at the beginning of the note on page 85 of the student's book may be used as examples. Exercise 50e gives practice in choice of the correct tense of the subjunctive.

11. It might be useful for the teacher to provide a *Building Up the Meaning* exercise (on the lines of that included in Chapter 47) for **rogāre**, e.g.:
    Mē pecūniam rogāvit.
    Mē rogāvit ut pecūniam sibi darem.
    Mē rogāvit ubi pecūnia esset.
Examples in primary as well as secondary sequence should be used, e.g.,
    Mē pecūniam rogat.
    Mē rogat ut pecūniam sibi dem.
    Mē rogat ubi pecūnia sit.

12. *Cicero: Coming of Age Ceremonies for Nephew and Son:* For background on Cicero, see *The Oxford Classical Dictionary*, pp. 234–238.

13. *Versiculī: "Nucēs Relinquere,"* pages 121–122
We include **decet**, which was introduced in Chapter 49, in the vocabulary list to show its principal parts; the subjunctive **deceat** is used in a clause of characteristic introduced by the indefinite **quodcunque** and may be translated by an indicative in English, e.g., "whatsoever is not fit for his years of manhood." In line 6, **nucēs** is a metaphor for childhood games. Note that **diēs** is feminine here, as it usually is when it refers to a specific day.

14. *Augury:* The remarks here on the taking of the omens are important for an understanding of the religious aspects of the three types of ceremony that we deal with in the last five chapters of this student's book. The passage from Livy illustrates exactly how the omens would be taken on an occasion of great public importance. For further information on augury, see *The Oxford Classical Dictionary*, "Augures," p. 147, "Auspicium," p. 154, "Divination," pp. 356–357, and "Haruspices," p. 489. The main ancient source of information is Cicero's *De divinatione*. For further information on Roman religion in general, see *Roman Religion and Roman Life*, "Roman Religion," pp. 340–353.

Language Activity Book

1. Activity 50a: See above, Student's Book, note 9. This exercise is based closely on the reading passage at the beginning of Chapter 50, and students should be allowed to use that passage in doing the exercise. The purpose of the exercise is to show how direct requests and commands are transformed into indirect.

Note that in Nos. 1 and 2 the future indicatives of the direct questions become imperfect subjunctives in the indirect commands. Here the imperfect subjunctives will indicate time *subsequent to* that of the main verb. Compare the general rules given for sequence of tenses on pages 77–78 of the student's book.

The following are sample translations of the sentences in Activity 50a:

1a. Cornēlius amīcīs clientibusque, "Veniētisne crās," inquit, "domum meam?"
1b. Cornēlius amīcōs clientēsque invītāvit ut domum suam crās venīrent.
2a. Aliīs domuī appropinquantibus iānitor, "Prōcēdētisne," inquit, "in domum?"
2b. Iānitor aliōs appropinquantēs rogāvit ut in domum prōcēderent.
3a. Aliīs domuī appropinquantibus iānitor, "In viā manēte!" inquit.
3b. Iānitor aliīs domuī appropinquantibus praecipiēbat ut in viā manērent.
4a. Aliī, quī spērābant Cornēlium sē ad cēnam invītātūrum esse, "Nōlī nōs dīmittere!" inquiunt.

4b. Hī iānitōrem ōrāvērunt nē sē dīmitteret.
5a. Eīs iānitor, "Discēdite statim!" inquit.
5b. Iānitor eīs imperāvit ut statim discēderent.
6a. Omnibus domum intrantibus Cornēlius, "Venīte," inquit, "in ātrium."
6b. Cornēlius omnēs domum intrantēs rogāvit ut in ātrium venīrent.
7a. Cornēlius servō, "Togam pūram Marcō indue!" inquit.
7b. Cornēlius servō imperāvit ut togam pūram Marcō indueret.
8a. Cornēlius eīs quī sē comitābantur, "Manēte," inquit, "extrā Tabulārium."
8b. Cornēlius eōs quī sē comitābantur rogāvit ut extrā Tabulārium manērent.
9a. Cornēlius multīs, "Cēnāte apud mē hodiē!" inquit.
9b. Cornēlius multōs invītāvit ut apud sē hodiē cēnārent.

2. Activities 50b and c: Students should never be led to think that any two words in a language will ever be exact synonyms or antonyms. This is why we use the word *approximately* in the directions for these activities. It is also why we ask students to give definitions for each word. For the subtle shades of meaning and usage that differentiate the words in some of these pairs, the teacher may consult the *Oxford Latin Dictionary*.

3. The passage to be translated into English in Activity 50d is longer than usual and will present a special challenge to most students. It is based closely on the passage from Livy quoted at the end of Chapter 50 in the student's book, and the Latin provided as a sample translation below is fairly close to Livy's Latin. Many of the words given in the list accompanying the passage will be familiar to the students from having met other, related words. The teacher may wish to stress the words for directions (right, left, north, south, east, and west). The grammar involved in this passage should be familiar enough to the students so that they will enjoy a considerable sense of accomplishment and achievement when they have completed the translation.

Note that "to his left" is **ad laevam** with the feminine noun **manum** omitted. Students should also be told that in the last sentence "when the signs were sent" should be translated with linking **quī**.

The following is a sample translation of the paragraph:

Numa Rōmam vocātus dē sē et dē regnō deōs cōnsulī iussit. Ab augure ductus in arcem in lapide ad merīdiem versus cōnsēdit. Augur ad laevam eius capite vēlātō sedem cēpit, dextrā manū baculum sine nōdīs tenēns, quem lituum appellāvērunt. Deinde prōspectū in urbem agrumque captō deōs precātus est et caelum ab oriente ad occāsum dētermināvit. Dextrās ad merīdiem partēs, laevās ad septentriōnem esse dīxit. Signum contrā animō fīnīvit. Tum lituō in laevam manum trānslātō dextram in caput Numae imposuit et ita precātus est, "Iuppiter pater, sī est fās hunc Numam Pompilium, cuius ego caput teneō, rēgem Rōmae esse, rogō ut tū signa nōbīs certa dēs inter eōs fīnēs quōs fēcī." Tum dīxit signa quae mittī vellet. Quibus missīs dēclārātus rēx Numa dē arce dēscendit.

CHAPTER 51: PAPIRIUS PRAETEXTATUS

Student's Book

1. a. No new grammar is introduced in this Chapter.
   b. The reading passage is essentially Gellius, *Noctes Atticae* I.23, with some changes and omissions to reduce the amount of new vocabulary and to make the various constructions clearer. Even so, some of the sentences are quite difficult for this stage of the course, and it is suggested that the teacher should be more willing than usual to help students over the difficulties rather than allow them to become frustrated through lack of success.

   The passage is given in its entirety, unadapted, with additional vocabulary and notes, as a translation exercise in the language activity book. After having read the adapted version in the student's book, students should be able to tackle the original text with confidence.

2. Words to be deduced: **praetextātus** (1), **introīre** (1–2), **mātrōna** (9), **perferre** (9), and **prūdentia** (18).

3. The passage provides good practice in several of the constructions presented in the fourth student's book:
   a. indirect command: 3, 11–12, and 16–17 (note the introductory verbs: **placuit**, 3, and **cōnsultum fēcit**, 16)
   b. indirect question; 4, 7–8, 12–13, and 14–15
   c. indirect statement: 5 and 7
   d. result: 6
   e. ablative absolute: 7

4. In this passage, the indirect commands are of a more difficult variety in which no specific person is given the instruction:
   Placuit nē quis. . . . (3)
   It was decided that no one should. . . .
   . . . ōrāvērunt ut ūna uxor. . . . (11)
   . . . they begged that one wife should. . . .
   . . . cōnsultum fēcit nē . . . puerī. . . . (16)
   (The senate) passed a decree that boys should not. . . .

5. The two indirect statements are of an impersonal variety in which no accusative subject is expressed:
   . . . respondit nōn licēre. . . . (5)
   (The boy) replied that it was not allowed. . . .
   Dīxit āctum esse. . . . (7)
   He said that it had been debated. . . .

In these examples, however, the insertion of "that" should carry the students over the difficulty.

The second indirect statement introduces an indirect question: "He said it had been debated *whether* . . . (7–8). The sense of the passage should lead to the translation "whether one man should have . . . or whether. . . ." This is the first example in the course of an alternative question with **utrum . . . an**.

6. **maior** (2): Here in the sense "rather important." Note also the comparative adverb **vehementius** in line 6.

7. **Māter Papiriī, puerī quī. . . .** (3): Teachers should guide students toward "the mother of Papirius" (rather than "Papirius' mother") to enable them to deal with **puerī** as genitive in apposition to **Papiriī**.

8. **prūdēns** (7); Technically, this adjective could agree with either **puer** or **cōnsilium**. Students should be asked to consider which fits the context better. Such a discussion will provide an opportunity to remind students that adjectives like **prūdēns** have the same form in the nominative singular of all three genders (cf. **ingēns**, **ēlegāns**, and all present participles like **sequēns**).

9. In line 13, **vellent** means "meant."

10. **tantam** (18): An example of **tantus** not followed by a result clause.

11. The expressions and **sententiae** at the bottom of page 92 of the student's book provide an opportunity to discuss the importance of custom and tradition in Roman life (see *The Romans*, "The Old Ways," pp. 14–26).

12. Exercise 51a is longer and more challenging than usual for this type of exercise in the student's book. Some or all of it may be assigned for written work. The following are sample translations of the sentences:
   1. Mōs puerīs Rōmānīs praetextātīs fuit cum patribus in Cūriam introīre.
   2. Ōlim senātōrēs rem maiōrem agēbant.
   3. Placuit ut rēs in diem posterum prōferrētur.
   4. Senātōrēs imperāvērunt nē rēs ēnūntiārētur.
   5. Māter Papīriī rogāvit fīlium quid ā senātōribus āctum esset.
   6. Puer respondit sē rem nōn ēnūntiātūrum esse.
   7. Eō magis silentium puerī mātrem incitāvit.
   8. Puer, mātre urgente, ēnūntiāvit senātōrēs agere utrum vir ūnam uxōrem an duās habēret.
   9. Quō audītō, māter Papīriī domō ēgressa est.
   10. Rem cum cēterīs mātrōnīs agēbat.
   11. Placuit ut caterva mātrōnārum ad Cūriam postrīdiē īret.
   12. Trepidantēs ōrāvērunt ut ūnus vir ūnam uxōrem potius quam duās habēret.
   13. Senātōrēs mīrābantur cūr fēminae hoc dīcerent.
   14. Papīrius ēnūntiāvit quid mātrī dīxisset.

15. Ingenium puerī senātōrēs adeō incitāvit ut cōnsultum facerent ut posteā Papīrium sōlum in Cūriam cum patre introīret.
16. Honōris causā eī dedērunt cognōmen Praetextātum.

13. *Roman Names:* For further information, see *Roman Life*, pp. 110−113, for family relationships, and the Chapter "Roman Names," pp. 116−125.

14. *Roman Weddings II:* For further background information on Roman weddings, see the references above, Chapter 49, Student's Book, note 12 on *Roman Weddings I.*

The custom of a girl's dedicating her toys to the household gods on the evening before her wedding may seem more credible if it is kept in mind that the girl is still likely to be a child in years and not yet a woman of an age that we would consider appropriate for marriage. She may have been playing with the toys even the day before her wedding. The contrast with modern customs may evoke comments from students.

Generally speaking, Roman marriages could be described as political, in the sense that they were arranged for the mutual advantage of the two families concerned within the larger framework of the familial networks (**amīcitia** and **clientēla**) that made Roman society work. See *The Roman Revolution,* Chapter 2. One of the major concerns of the groom's family was to secure an heir in the form of a grandson to inherit and perpetuate the wealth of the family. Again, contrasts with modern customs may evoke comments from students.

The word **mundus**, often occurring in the phrase **mundus muliebris**, is of uncertain etymology (perhaps Etruscan), but the ancient grammarian Varro (*De lingua Latina* 5.129) derived it from the Latin **munditia, -ae** (*f*), cleanliness, elegance, refinement.

According to Cicero (see the quotation at the end of the previous chapter), in earlier times virtually no act was started without taking the auspices; by Cicero's day, however, the **auspex**, though always present at a wedding, did not perform his function as an **augur**, but merely acted as a kind of registrar or witness. This would suggest that divination gradually fell into disuse as time went on, but we can be sure that Cornelius, being one of the old school of Romans, would wish to have the ceremony carried out according to true Roman tradition.

Language Activity Book

1. Activity 51a: See note 1 above. The following are sample translations of the five Latin paragraphs:
1. Previously it was the custom for Roman senators to enter the Senate House with their sons (who were still) wearing the **toga praetexta**. At a time when a certain rather important matter had been discussed and delayed until the next day and when it was decided that no one should announce the matter about which they were carrying on a discussion before it had been settled, the mother of Papirius, a boy who had been in the Senate House with his father, asked her son what the senators had debated in the senate.
2. The boy replied that he had to be silent and that it was not permitted that it (the matter) be told. The woman becomes more desirous of hearing; the secret of the matter and the silence of the boy stir up her mind to asking; she therefore asks more urgently and violently. Then the boy, since his mother was urging, forms a plan (consisting) of a clever and witty lie.
3. He said it was debated in the senate whether it seemed more useful and in the interests of the state that one man should have two wives or that one (wife) should be married with two (men). When she heard this, her mind became fearful, in a panic she goes out of the house, she reports (it) to other matrons.
4. On the next day a crowd of matrons came to the senate. Weeping and beseeching they beg that one (woman) should rather be married to two (men) than that two (women) to one (man). The senators, coming into the Senate House, were wondering what that outrageous behavior of the women and what that demand meant.
5. The boy Papirius, having come forward into the middle of the Senate House, told the matter just as it had been—what his mother had insisted on hearing (and) what he himself had said to his mother. The senate expressed great admiration for the loyalty and ingenuity of the boy; it made a decree that henceforth boys not enter the Senate House with their fathers except that one Papirius, and that afterwards the boy be given the nickname "Praetextatus" as an honor on account of his wisdom of keeping quiet and speaking at his youthful age.

2. Activity 51b: The following are hints of answers to the questions on the passage:
1. The answer should emphasize the mother's curiosity and vehemence.
2. The answer should include reference to how the narrator makes the boy's lie seem a clever and playful way out of the bind he is put in by his mother's insistence that he tell the secret.
3. **animus compavēscit, trepidāns, lacrimantēs, obsecrantēs.** The word **intemperiēs** best characterizes their behavior and suggests an anti-feminine bias.
4. **exōsculātur.**
5. **fidem, ingenium,** and **prūdentiam.**
6. These questions should spark lively discussion and debate with no need to arrive at final answers.
7. Students might mention the emotionalism and panic of the women and the clear-headed actions of the men, though some may characterize

the senators' behavior as reactionary emotionalism.

8. In answering this question, students might consider the moral, familial, and societal questions involved in the situation in which Papirius is put in the bind of being able to keep the secret and maintain his loyalty to his father (the pillar of the family) and to the senate (Roman society in microcosm) only by lying and deceiving his mother. Which is shown to be more important, obedience to his mother or loyalty to his father and (through his father) to the senators? Why is loyalty to his father and the senators of greater importance to Papirius? Why does he unquestioningly speak for his father when his mother's insistence provokes a critical moment of decision? What are the respective roles and positions of the father and mother within the family and within the larger community? To what extent can the episode be seen as a conflict between society (organized along strictly patriarchal lines) and what a Roman male would consider a prying busybody (or busybodies, if the other **mātrōnae** are included)?

WORD STUDY XIII

1. The aims of this section are:
   a. to show that Latin is the major source of the five national Romance languages: French, Italian, Spanish, Portuguese, and Rumanian
   b. to illustrate the interrelationship among these Romance languages
   c. to explain some of the changes that took place in the development of the Romance languages from Latin.

2. The relationship of Latin to the Romance languages is too vast a topic to allow comprehensive treatment in this Word Study. Instead, a few of the more salient points are briefly presented, allowing students to shape their own impressions of this relationship by working through the exercises that follow.

   For a comprehensive study of this subject, see *The Story of Latin and the Romance Languages*. Also useful is this brief summary by Ronald Palma of the Holland Hall School, Tulsa, Oklahoma:

   Latin, the language of Rome, was at the outset only one of many local dialects of Latium. It takes its name from the Latini, a people derived from the tribes of Indo-Europeans who migrated to the peninsula around 1000 B.C. Latin's early development was influenced by Celtic inroads from the north, by Greeks from the south, and by Etruscans in north-central Italy. Subsequently, the expansion of Latin followed the advance of Roman conquest in the Mediterranean and, carried by the Roman army throughout the Empire, became a major vehicle for the Romanization of conquered peoples. Latin displaced native languages almost everywhere except in the East, where Greek remained dominant.

   Derived from the Roman tongue, there developed in Europe the various regional languages of French, Italian, Portuguese, Spanish, and Rumanian, called *Romance* languages (from the word "Roman").

   The Romance derivatives of Latin are currently spoken by more than 600 million people, in the following order by number of native speakers: Spanish, Portuguese, French, Italian, and Rumanian. These languages developed from colloquial or popular Latin (**sermō plēbēius**), also called "vulgar" Latin (the Latin of the **vulgus**, or crowd), rather than from the formal Latin of classical authors. A glimpse at the "man-on-the-street" Latin in Plautus and later in Petronius shows a simpler grammatical structure than formal Latin, and a speech filled with idiomatic expressions and slang. One factor contributing to the decentralization of Latin and the spread of vernacular languages was the split of the Roman Empire around A.D. 300, into a mostly Latin-speaking western half and a mostly Greek-speaking eastern half. The collapse of the western Roman Empire in the 5th century brought about the final loss of centralization and the virtual extinction of literary Latin in the West. By A.D. 600, rapid regionalization of Latin was occurring, leading ultimately to the variations of the modern Romance languages.

   At least 90% of the vocabulary of the Romance languages is derived (from **dē** + **rīvus**, "flow from") from Latin. Note the similarities below:

ENGLISH:	Give us this day our daily bread.
LATIN:	Da nōbīs hodiē pānem nostrum quotidiānum.
SPANISH:	Da nos hoy nuestro pan cotidiano.
PORTUGUESE:	O pao nosso de cada dia dainos hoje.
FRENCH:	Donne-nous aujourd'hui notre pain quotidien.
ITALIAN:	Dacci oggi il nostro pane cotidiano.

3. The chart on page 39 illustrates the development of the Indo-European family of languages. Note that, since its organization is primarily vertical, the chart does not show the possible horizontal influence of one language on another, e.g., the influence of Greek on Latin, or French on English. The chart also shows graphically how some English words, seemingly derived from Latin, are actually cognates of Latin words, i.e., they come from the same Indo-European parent; e.g., *name* and **nōmen**, *have* and **habeō**. This chart may be duplicated and distributed to students.

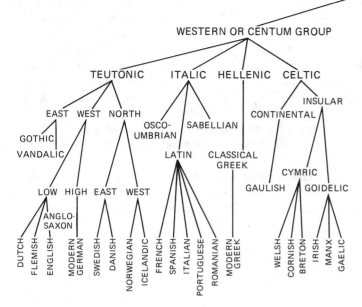

Indo-European Parent Language

WESTERN OR CENTUM GROUP — TEUTONIC, ITALIC, HELLENIC, CELTIC

EASTERN OR SATEM GROUP — BALTO-SLAVIC, INDO-IRANIAN, ARMENIAN, ALBANIAN

4. In Exercise 1, students (with the aid of the teacher) should be encouraged to attempt pronunciation of the words in French, Italian, and Spanish. Teachers unsure of the correct pronunciation should consult modern language dictionaries and/or colleagues in the modern languages before attempting this exercise with students.

5. Exercise 2 illustrates the worldwide influence of Latin, through its three most ubiquitous descendants: Spanish, Portuguese, and French. The following is a list of the places (other than the homeland) where these languages are spoken today:

SPANISH: Argentina, Bolivia, Chile, Colombia, Ecuador, Paraguay, Peru, Uruguay, Venezuela, Guatemala, El Salvador, Costa Rica, Honduras, Nicaragua, Panama, Mexico, the West Indies, Cuba, Santo Domingo, Puerto Rico, the Philippines, southwestern United States.

PORTUGUESE: Brazil; islands of Madeira, Azores, Cape Verde; former colonies in Asia, e.g., Macao; former colonies in Africa, e.g., Angola.

FRENCH: Belgium, Switzerland, Quebec (Canada), French Guiana; several Caribbean islands, e.g., Haiti; some Pacific Islands, e.g., New Caledonia; former colonies in Africa, e.g., Morocco, Algeria, Ivory Coast, Senegal, Madagascar; former colonies in Southeast Asia, e.g., Cambodia, Vietnam.

6. Exercise 2 can serve as the springboard to student projects, such as the construction of a world map, color-coded to indicate areas where Romance languages are spoken. Further information and sample maps may be found in Chapter 19 of *The Story of Latin and the Romance Languages.*

7. The ideas presented in this Word Study section suggest the possibility of joint activities with students of modern languages, e.g.:

a. Write a list of school rules in simultaneous translation from English to Latin, French, Spanish, etc. This could also be done for a collection of school cheers, the school alma mater, the cafeteria menu, or even a love-letter.

b. Write and perform a short play using a familiar plot (e.g., a fairy tale), first in Latin, then in French, Spanish, etc. (If a familiar plot is used, the audience will already have a good idea of what is being said.)

c. Write and perform Latin, French, Spanish, etc. translations of a popular song. (The popularity of the song should insure that the audience is already familiar with the lyrics in English.)

CHAPTER 52: CORNELIA'S WEDDING

Student's Book

1. a. This Chapter introduces purpose clauses.
   b. The account of Cornelia's wedding follows the pattern of the description of Roman weddings on page 95 of the student's book. The **versiculī** keyed to this Chapter consist of extracts from a wedding hymn of Catullus, and we recommend that they be read after study of the story, the grammar, and Exercise 52b and before the

stories about Arria. The latter stories shift the focus from the joys of the wedding ceremonies to the harder realities of married life including the demands made upon a wife by her connubial devotion in times of crises involving sickness and death. The stories describe the illness of Arria's husband, the death and funeral of their son, and the suicides of Arria and her husband. The themes of death lead to the background note on Roman funerals and to the subject of the final Chapter of the book.

2. Words to be deduced: **sacrificāre** (11), **hilaritās** (16), and **praecēdere** (19).

3. The two purpose clauses introduced by **ut** (2−3 and 11) can both be translated by the English infinitive, as was the case with the indirect commands introduced in Chapter 50 (see above, Chapter 50, Student's Book, note 2). The example with **nē** (22) is given in the vocabulary.

4. Notes on vocabulary and grammar:
  a. **tunicam albam indūta** (7): The perfect passive participle is not used in this idiom in a passive sense but rather with the force of a Greek middle voice in which the participle has an active meaning, takes a direct object, and implies a dative of reference referring to the subject of the participle: "*having put* a white tunic *on herself.* For other constructions with this verb, see 41:22 and 50:25.
  b. **sacrīs rīte parātīs** (10): No one word can adequately translate the neuter plural **sacra**, which became a noun in its own right: **sacra, -ōrum** (*n pl*). The word would conjure up a whole host of ideas: the sacred vessels and utensils, and the ritual cleansing of these; incense; ribbons; salt and meal; the acts of standing in a set order and facing in a certain direction; as well as the actual offering itself. An inclusive translation such as the following may be suggested: "when all the preparations for the religious ceremony had been duly made."
  c. **simulābat sē eam. . . .** (17−18): This is a useful sentence to point out the difference between **sē** and **is, ea, id**.
  d. **nova nūpta** (21): We give the translation of this stock phrase, and we also give a full entry for the verb from which the noun comes. The verb is an important one for students to know, and they should be aware of the relationship between the verb and the noun.
  e. **sublāta est** (22): Students should be reminded of the principal parts of this verb, **tollō, tollere** (3), **sustulī, sublātum**, and of its meaning, "to lift," "to raise."

5. Lines 10−14 are suitable for dictation.

6. *Purpose Clauses:* The teacher should state explicitly that in English we commonly express purpose by the infinitive, whereas the Romans used **ut** or **nē** and the subjunctive. (See above, Chapter 50, Student's Book, note 8, for a similar recommendation concerning indirect commands.) It is especially important that students remember this when translating from English to Latin and when responding to Latin questions. In studying the subordinate constructions in Latin it is important that students recognize that some linguistic features are unique to particular languages; there is no better way to illustrate this than to contrast the constructions used in Latin and in English to express the same idea.

The **sententiae** and the epigram of Martial are quoted for their use of purpose clauses. The macron is omitted from **mittō** in the epigram because the *o* must be read as a short vowel here for purposes of the meter.

7. Versiculī: "Bridal Hymn," pages 122−123: A translation of the greater part of the poem from which these extracts are taken will be found in the cultural background readings on pages 50−52 of this handbook and may be read to the students either before or after working on the Latin extracts.
  a. Words to be deduced: **Ōceanus** (4) and **hyacinthinus** (8).
  b. In the last stanza, the word **nucēs** has both a literal meaning (for the throwing of nuts at weddings, see the end of the note on page 95 of the student's book) and a metaphorical meaning (see **Versiculī** 28 with the metaphorical use of **nucēs** = "childhood games" in the last line).

8. *A Noble Wife:* The version of this story in the student's book is quite close to Pliny's original. The latter is given with additional vocabulary aid as a translation exercise in the language activity book (Activity 52b).
  a. Words to be deduced: **pulchritūdō** (2), **interrogāre** (5), and **prōrumpere** (7).
  b. **aegrōtābat et fīlius** (1): As not many examples of **et** meaning "too" have occurred, students may need some help with this.
  c. **eximiā pulchritūdine** (2): The ablative of description will be treated formally in the fifth student's book (an example appeared in Exercise 37e, line 10). It may cause difficulty, but the clue of **et** followed by **parentibus cārissimus** should help students to realize that these two phrases are essentially parallel ideas and that both describe **puer** (2).
  d. **cum . . . intrāverat** (4): **Cum** has appeared once before (30:5−6) in a general temporal clause (= "whenever"). There it was used with the perfect indicative (". . . whenever a Roman senator invites. . . ."), and here it is used with the pluperfect indicative (". . . whenever she entered. . . .").
  e. Structures:
  Word order:
    Aegrōtābat Caecina. . . . (1)

... **ignōrāret marītus.** (3–4)
... **vīvere fīlium.** ... (4–5)
... **Paetō saepe interrogantī ... respondēbat,** .... (5–6)
... **quid ageret puer,** .... (5–6)
Anaphora:
Aegrōtābat Caecina ..., **aegrōtābat et fīlius** .... (1)
... **ita fūnus parāvit, ita dūxit exsequiās** .... (3)
List:
... **lacrimās retinēbat, dolōrem operiēbat.** (9)

9. *Another Story about Arria:* With the theme of the suicide of the devoted wife here one may compare the story of Pyramus and Thisbe. The reversal of the order of the suicides here emphasizes the nobility and courage of Arria.

10. *Roman Funerals:* With the funeral rituals described here the teacher may compare those described by Vergil in the funeral of Misenus in the heroic age of the *Aeneid;* see the passages quoted on pages 52–53 of the cultural background readings at the end of this handbook.

For further background information, see the following:
   a. *Roman Religion,* pp. 12–13.
   b. *Roman Family Life,* "A Death in the Family," pp. 55–62, and the accompanying *Aspects of Roman Life Folder A* (white card 5.16, "Death in the Family," and yellow source card 1.32, "Death").
   c. *Rome: Its People, Life and Customs,* "Funeral Rites," pp. 128–133.
   d. *Roman Life,* "The Romans and Their Dead," pp. 354–373.
   e. *Death and Burial in the Roman World,* "Funerary Rites and the Cult of the Dead," pp. 43–64.

Language Activity Book

1. Activity 52b: The following are sample translations of the two paragraphs of this story:
   1. Caecina Paetus, the husband of Arria, was ill, (their) son was ill, both mortally, as it seemed. The son died, (a boy) of outstanding beauty (and) equal modesty, and dear to (his) parents no less for other (reasons) than that he was (their) son. She prepared his funeral and carried out the funeral rites in such a way that (her) husband was ignorant (of it); indeed whenever she entered his bedroom, she pretended that (their) son was still alive and even in better health, and to (her husband) who was very often asking how the boy was doing she would reply, "He rested well, he took food willingly."
   2. Then when the tears that she had held back for a long time overcame (her) and burst forth, she went out (from her husband's sick room); then

she gave herself over to grief; satiated (i.e., when her grief was exhausted) with her eyes dried and face composed she would return, as if she had left the loss of her child outside the door. She hid (her) tears, covered (her) mourning, and although she had lost her son she still acted the mother.

2. Activity 52c: The teacher may prepare students for writing the assigned essay by conducting a class discussion on Arria, the mother of Papirius, and Roman women in general. This might help generate ideas, focus issues, and narrow down particular themes on which students could write.

Alternatively, students might be offered the names of other Roman women to research and be asked to write comparisons of their characters and lives with those of women today. The depth of such an assignment would depend on the age and the ability of the class.

For general background on Roman women, see *Goddesses, Whores, Wives, and Slaves: Women in Classical Antiquity,* "The Roman Matron of the Late Republic and Early Empire," pp. 149–189. For a rich variety of specific source material (epitaphs, inscriptions, and passages from ancient writers), see *Women's Life in Greece & Rome: A Source Book in Translation,* "Wives, Mothers, Daughters," pp. 133–156.

CHAPTER 53: A SAD OCCASION

Student's Book

1. a. No new grammar is formally introduced in this chapter.
   b. As well as bringing to an end the activities of the Cornelii, as far as this course is concerned, this Chapter provides review of the main subordinate constructions that have been learned in the fourth book. The note on translating **ut** should help students cope with this subordinating conjunction in a systematic way.
   c. The Latin words that occur in the note on Roman funerals on page 103 of the student's book are important for translation of the reading passage in Chapter 53 and should be known by students before they begin the story.

As Titus was a person of some importance, we have given him a public funeral, and this connects with the Polybius passage that follows. The Chapter also contains sample epitaphs of real Romans and notes on funeral customs; it concludes with Catullus' moving poem on the last rites at his brother's grave.

2. Words to be deduced: **lūbricus** (9), **medicus** (10), **incidere** (12), **vīta** (14), **excēdere** (15), **postrēmus** (22), **impōnere** (27), **āvertere** (29), and **inicere** (29).

3. Examples of all of the subordinate constructions except **cum** causal occur in this passage. After the passage has been read and comprehended, teachers

may ask students to identify examples of the following in sequence in the passage (the constructions are listed in the order in which they are presented in the fourth student's book, and not in their order of occurrence in the passage):

    a. **cum** circumstantial clauses
    b. indirect questions
    c. ablative absolutes
    d. indirect statements
    e. result clauses
    f. indirect commands
    g. **iubeō** + infinitive
    h. purpose clauses
    i. **ut** + indicative

4. Notes on vocabulary and grammar:

    a. est arcessendus (10): Treat this example of a passive periphrastic as a vocabulary item; the construction will be formally presented in the fifth student's book.

    b. convalēscere . . . ingravēscēbat (11–13): Students may be reminded of the discussion of inceptive verbs in Word Study XII on page 69 of the student's book.

    c. familiārēs (22): See above, Chapter 50, Student's Book, note 5e on **familiam** (50:15) and **Laribus familiāribus** (50:23). In 53:22 the word **familiārēs** is used as a noun referring to close friends outside the immediate family.

    d. iniēcit (29): It should be noted that, in this context, **iniēcit** means "thrust in," not "threw in."

5. Structures:

    a. Verb and subject inverted:
        . . . **accidit rēs trīstissima** (3)
        . . . **audītae sunt vōcēs.** . . . (5)
        . . . **ardēbant lucernae.** . . . (18)
        Praecēdēbant tubicinēs. (19)
        . . . **Subsequēbantur mulierēs** . . . (20)
        . . . **impositum est corpus.** . . . (27)
        Appropinquāvit . . . Cornēlius. . . . (28)

    b. List: (19–22)

    c. Condensed sentence:
        Commemorāvit quālis . . ., quot. . . . (24)
        Commemorābant quam . . . , quantum. . . . (31)

    d. Linking **quī:**
        Quam taedam. . . . (29)

6. Exercise 53a: Note that all of the subordinate clauses in this exercise are in primary sequence rather than secondary sequence as in the story. This is a good opportunity to review the concept of sequence of tenses. The following are sample translations:

    1. Aestāte calor in urbe tantus est ut omnēs ad vīllam redīre velint.

    2. Gāius Cornēlius igitur in animō habet omnia parāre ut Bāiās redeant.

    3. Cornēlius, ut solet, cum Titō frātre ad balneās it.

    4. "Cavē! Pavīmentum tam lēve et lūbricum est ut cadās."

    5. Subitō servōs urget ut lectīcam in domum ferant.

    6. Titus iam tam īnfirmus est ut vix loquī possit.

    7. In Forō Cornēlius commemorat quot merita Titus in prīncipem cīvēsque contulerit.

    8. Exsequiīs cōnfectīs, Cornēliī commemorant quam hilaris Titus fuerit, quantum līberōs amāverit.

7. *Epitaphs*

    a. Words to be deduced: **monumentum** (*ii*), **līberta** (*iii*), **violāre** (*iv*), **recipere** (*iv*), **pellege** = **perlege** (*v*), and **locāre** (*v*). Grammar to be deduced: ablatives of description in line 7 of *v*.

    b. Students will enjoy identifying the deviations from standard spelling in *v*. They are **deicō** (= **dīcō**), **paullum** (= **paulum**), **astā** (= **adstā**), **pellege** (= **perlege**), **heic** (= **hīc**), **pulcrum** (= **pulchrum**), **pulcrai** (= **pulchrae**), **nōminārunt** (= **nōmināvērunt**), **suom** (= **suum**), **mareitum** (= **marītum**), **deilēxit** (= **dīlēxit**), **souō** (= **suō**), **gnātōs** (= **nātōs**), **hōrunc** (= **hōrum**), and **abei** (= **abī**). Note that **quod** (1) means "what."

    c. The fifth epitaph tells much about the character and personality of the deceased woman and should provoke considerable discussion, following up on the discussion of Roman women recommended in conjunction with Activity 52c in the language activity book (see above, Chapter 52, Language Activity Book, note 2). What do the spellings in the inscription tell us about the social and educational level of Claudia's family? What were Claudia's main concerns and values? What did her husband (if that is the person who wrote the inscription) appreciate and value in her?

    d. Students may be asked to compose (in Latin or in English) an epitaph for Titus.

8. Exercise 53b: Some students would enjoy completing the sentences in this exercise.

9. *At a Brother's Grave:* This justifiably famous poem of Catullus may cause some problems for students in translation, but we have tried to be as generous as necessary with vocabulary aids. To be deduced: **alloquī** (4), **fortūna** (5), and **frāternus** (9). The poem should provoke discussion of the rituals involved in memorial services at the grave and the relationship between those rituals and the feelings and emotions of the bereaved. Alliteration of *m*s is particularly effective in this poem and deliberately calls attention to words for death, the ashes of the dead, the ritual offerings, and the tears of the speaker.

10. Versiculī: "Martial Laughs over Illness and Death." The first words of the third epigram are conventional and found on many epitaphs. They are often abbreviated **S.T.T.L.** Other frequent sepulchral abbreviations are **H.I.S. (hīc iacet sepultus** or **situs), H.M.P. (hoc monumentum posuit), D.M. (dīs mānibus),** and **R.I.P. (requiēscat in pāce).**

Language Activity Book

1. Activity 53a: This letter of Pliny (V.16) will be a challenge to most students at this level. The teacher may need to provide more help than usual, but as with the poem of Catullus in the student's book, we have tried to provide notes for all unfamiliar vocabulary, grammar, and cultural background. The content of the letter is very appropriate to the stories in the second half of *Pastimes and Ceremonies*; note the themes of childhood, marriage, illness, and death as they occur in the stories and as they occur in this letter.

The following are sample translations of the paragraphs of the letter:

1. Gaius Pliny greets his friend Aefulanus Marcellinus. I write this to you very sadly because the younger daughter of our (friend) Fundanus has died. I have never seen anyone (literally, anything) more congenial, more lovable, and more worthy not only of a longer life but almost of immortality than that girl.

2. She had not yet filled out 14 years, and already she had the wisdom of an old woman, the seriousness of a married woman, and at the same time (literally, nevertheless) a girlish charm (along) with maidenly modesty. How she clung to her father's neck! How lovingly and modestly she embraced us friends of her father! What special regard she had for her wet-nurses, her tutors, and her private instructors, each according to his (her) own responsibility! How eagerly, how intelligently she was in the habit of reading! How moderately and cautiously she jested!

3. With what self-control, with what endurance, with even what resolution she bore her last illness! She followed the orders of her doctors, she encouraged her sister and father, and she sustained herself by the power of her will when deprived of bodily strength. This (the power of her will) remained for her right up to the end, nor was it broken by either the length of (her) illness or by fear of death, so that (as a result of all of this) she left us more and deeper causes of longing and grief.

4. O utterly sad and untimely funeral! O time of death more cruel than death itself! Already she had been promised to an outstanding young man, already the wedding day had been chosen, already we had been invited. What joy was exchanged for what mourning! I am not able to express in words what a great wound I received in my spirit when I heard Fundanus himself, as his grief found many sorrowful things, giving orders (that) the money which he had been about to pay for clothing, pearls, and gems be spent (instead) for frankincense, unguents, and perfumes.

5. To be sure he is well-educated and philosophical, since from earliest youth he devoted himself to higher studies and liberal arts; but now he rejects all the things which he often heard and often said, and with all his other virtuous qualities driven out he is totally given over to his compassionate feelings (for his child). You will pardon (him), you will even praise (him), if you think of what he has lost.

6. For he lost a daughter who recalled no less his character than (his) face and expression and entirely resembled (her) father with remarkable similarity. Accordingly if you send him any letter about (his) very legitimate grief, remember to offer consolation not as if (i.e., that is not) full of reproof and too severe, but gentle and humane.

7. A long length of intervening time will bring it about that he will accept it (i.e., your consolation) more easily (than he will right now). For as a fresh wound recoils from the hands of doctors, (but) then (as it heals) puts up with and even seeks (the hands of doctors) voluntarily, so fresh grief of the spirit rejects and shrinks away from consolations, (but) soon desires (them) and finds comfort in them if they are offered gently. Farewell!

2. Activity 53b: Most students will find these questions challenging, especially the ones dealing with stylistic effects. Most of the latter, however, have been encountered frequently in the notes on structure in the reading passages and in the **versiculī**. The teacher should be available and willing to offer help as needed to students in answering the questions in Activity 53b, just as the teacher should offer any needed help to students in translating the letter in Activity 53a.

REVIEW XII

Student's Book

1. The main grammatical features in Chapters 49–53 that require review are:
   a. Result clauses
   b. Sequence of tenses
   c. Indirect commands
   d. Purpose clauses
   e. Use of **ut** with the indicative ("as" or "when") and with the subjunctive (in result clauses, indirect commands, and purpose clauses)

2. Exercise XIIa: The same comments apply as for Exercise XIa; see above Review XI, Student's Book, note 2. Again, teachers may wish to do some of the sentences in class and assign others for written work.

3. Exercise XIIb:
   a. Words to be deduced: **occāsiō** (3), **cantābundus** (7), **numerāre** (8), **iocārī** (9), **ululāre** (11), and

lapideus (13). Note that **umbra**, which was used in Exercise 29g in the plural of the "shadows" or clients who came along uninvited with their masters to a **cēna**, is here used of the "shades" of the dead (14). **Ante**, previously used as a preposition (34:8), is here used as an adverb (15).

  b. **Quod** causal with the subjunctive (15) should cause no problems for students to translate: "My Melissa was wondering (was surprised) that I was walking so late." The two contrary-to-fact clauses with the pluperfect subjunctive (15 and 22) are translated in the vocabulary and will not cause students any trouble.

Language Activity Book

1. Activity RXIIa: Teachers are reminded that the English-Latin vocabulary on pages 62−64 of this handbook may be duplicated and made available to students as needed to assist in translation of the sentences in this activity.

The following are sample translations of the sentences in Activity RXIIa:

  1. Dominus meus Capuam vēnerat ut unguentum emeret.
  2. Ut mihi occāsiōnem ita dedit, amīcam Melissam vīsitāre cōnstituī.
  3. Cum sōlus īre timērem (verērer), rogāvī ut amīcus mēcum īret.
  4. Ut amīcus inter stēlās ambulābat, subitō lupus factus est.
  5. Tam perterritus eram ut anima in nāsō fuerit et tamquam mortuus steterim.
  6. Quid accidisset (factum esset) intellegere nōn poteram.
  7. Ad stēlās procēdō ut vestīmenta amīcī tollam.
  8. Tam celeriter currō ut brevī tempore ad vīllam amīcae meae perveniam.
  9. Mīrātur quid faciam et cūr hūc illūc hōc tempore noctis concursem.
  10. Mihi dīcit lupum vīllam intrāvisse et omnia pecora necāre cōnātum esse; deinde mē dēfessum hortātur ut quiēscam et obdormiam.

Addenda to Bibliography

BACKGROUND READINGS

The following books provide further useful background for the cultural topics treated in Book 3:

A History of Private Life: I: From Pagan Rome to Byzantium, ed. by Paul Veyne, tr. by Arthur Goldhammer. Harvard University Press, Cambridge, Massachusetts, 1987. ix + 670 pp.

> In particular:
> "Marriage," pp. 33–49.

As the Romans Did: A Sourcebook in Roman Social History, by Jo-Ann Shelton. Oxford University Press, New York, 1988. xix + 492 pp., paperback.

> In particular:
> "Baths," pp. 311–314, "Recitations," pp. 319–322, "Gambling and Gaming," p. 309, "Amphitheater Events," pp. 342–349, "Marriage," pp. 37–58, "Women in Roman Society," pp. 290–307, and "Funerary Laws and Funerals," pp. 97–101.

Civilization of the Ancient Mediterranean: Greece and Rome, ed. by Michael Grant and Rachel Kitzinger. 3 vols. Charles Scribner's Sons, New York, 1988.

> In particular:
> "Divination and Oracles: Rome," Vol. II, pp. 951–958; "Sacrifice and Ritual: Rome," Vol. II, pp. 981–986; "Roman Games," Vol. II, pp. 1153–1165; "Roman Marriage," Vol. III, pp. 1343–1354.

"The Colosseum," a 25" x 34" color reconstruction of the Colosseum at the time of Constantine. American Classical League, Miami University, Oxford, OH.

TEACHER'S AIDS

The American Classical League offers packets of mimeographs, many of which are useful to teachers of ECCE ROMANI. The following packets of mimeographs contain items of use in teaching Book 4:

M2. Mimeos on First Year Latin.
M3. Mimeos on Latin Club, Projects, and Games.
M4. Mimeos on Plays, Productions, and Readings in English and Latin.
M6. Mimeos on Rome and the Romans.
M7. Mimeos on Teaching Methods and Techniques.
M8. Mimeos on Value of the Classics.
M9. Mimeos on Word Study and Derivation.

Each mimeo is identified by a number, and some mimeos are included in more than one packet. The mimeos are not available individually, but only as packets. The following mimeos, identified by packet code and mimeo number, are particularly useful in teaching Book 4:

"Roman Baths," by M. Bentley (M3 and 6 #202): additional background information for Book 4, Chapter 41, "At the Baths."

"Pyramus and Thisbe" (M4 #487): a humorous skit in English to be read or performed after students have read the adapted version of the story in Book 4, Chapter 43, "Pyramus and Thisbe," and the selections in Latin from the original version in Ovid in the accompanying chapter of the language activity book.

"Rota: An Old Roman Game" (M3 #152): instructions for playing an ancient game, similar to our tick-tac-toe; a game students can try their hands at while reading about children's games in Book 4, Chapter 44, "A Rainy Day."

"A Short List of Latin Suffixes" (M7 and 9 #385): a convenient chart listing noun and adjective suffixes and giving the meaning of the suffix, examples of Latin words formed with the suffix, the meanings of these Latin words, and English derivatives. This list may be used with Book 4, pp. 67–69, "Word Study XII," as a convenient review of all the noun and adjective suffixes presented in the word study sections up to this point in the Latin course.

"A Brief Description of the Marriage Ceremonies of the Romans," by Marguerite Kretschmer (M3 and 6 #411): the different types of marriage, betrothal ceremonies, and a description of marriage customs and rites; with Book 4, Chapters 49, 51, and 52, dealing with the marriage of Cornelia and Valerius.

"Roman Dress," by Fannie Sherman (M3 and 6 #63): men's clothing, cloaks, and other wraps, women's clothing (including the bride's dress), special costumes, jewelry and other accessories, and miscellaneous items of interest; appropriate for study along with Book 4, Chapters 49, 51, and 52 on the wedding and Chapter 50 on Marcus' coming of age.

"A Roman Family Comes to Life" (M2, 4, and 6 #649): a skit in English that brings a Roman family to life and touches on many of the cultural topics treated in Book 4; appropriate for teaching after the coming of age ceremony in Book 4, Chapter 50.

"Latin in Romance Languages" (M2, 7, 8, and 9 #742): 251 Latin words with their Italian, Spanish, and French derivatives and their English meanings (or English derivatives); a convenient list to supplement Book 4, pp. 96–97, "Word Study XIII: Latin and the Romance Languages."

"The Morning of the Wedding: A Roman Fashion Show for Girls," by Lillian Lawler (M4 #580): a detailed account suitable for production as a fashion show with careful attention to the dress, hair styles, and jewelry of the bride, slaves, bride's mother, bride's best friend, her little sister, and the **prōnuba**; with Book 4, Chapter 52, "Cornelia's Wedding."

"Latin Words Adopted into English," by Clarence Gleason (M2 and 7 #446): a list of Latin words adopted without change of spelling into English; a useful word study unit that can be used at the end of Book 4.

The following book will be of use to teachers who wish to enrich the Latin course with material on English grammar:

English Grammar for Students of Latin, by Norma Goldman and Ladislas Szymanski. The Olivia and Hill Press, Inc., P.O. Box 7396, Ann Arbor, MI 48107. 1983. 6 + 202 pp.

The topics in the following sections of this book will be of particular use in teaching Book 4 of ECCE ROMANI:

What is an Infinitive?
What is the Subjunctive Mood?
What are Sentences, Phrases and Clauses?
What is Meant by Direct and Indirect Statement?
What is Meant by Direct and Indirect Questions?

The Romans Speak for Themselves

For use of these supplementary readers along with the ECCE ROMANI Latin program, see the first teacher's handbook, page 67.

The following lessons in *The Romans Speak for Themselves: Book II* are keyed to the chapters or sections of ECCE ROMANI Book 4 that are given in parentheses:

Chapter 6. An Unexpected Bath at Trimalchio's
Petronius, *Satyricon* 72–73
(after Chapter 41)
Chapter 7. Alypius Catches Gladiator Fever
Augustine, *Confessions* VI.8
(after Chapter 48)
Chapter 8. The Wedding of Cato and Marcia
Lucan, *Civil War* II.350–373
(after Chapter 52)

Vocabularies

The Vocabulary at the end of the student's book includes all Latin words used in the stories, grammatical notes, and exercises in the student's book. It does not include words that appear only in the culture, word study, and review sections, nor does it include words that appear only in the **versiculī**. The numbers at the left refer to the chapter in which each new word first appears. Words without numbers at the left were introduced in the first, second, or third student's book (except for a few words that appear only in the review sections of the fourth student's book as words to be deduced; these are included in the end vocabulary; in case students need to look them up).

In the Vocabulary at the end of the student's book, the genitive singular of 3rd declension nouns and the principal parts of verbs are abbreviated as they appear in the *Oxford Latin Dictionary*. This system of abbreviation allows students to sound out the full sets of forms with ease and accuracy.

The vocabularies at the end of this teacher's handbook, which may be duplicated and made available to students, are for use in conjunction with Review sections X, XI, and XII, which follow Chapters 43, 48, and 53, respectively, and the English-Latin translation exercises in the language activity book.

The **Latin Vocabularies** (pages 57–58) are arranged alphabetically by part of speech, with a separate listing of miscellaneous phrases and words that, at this stage, need not be grouped into parts of speech. Asterisks indicate words to be mastered.

The **English–Latin Vocabulary** (pages 59–60) is provided to assist students in doing the English to Latin translations in the language activity book.

Cultural Background Readings

The Baths

Lucius Annaeus Seneca (c. 4 B.C.–A.D. 65), tutor to Nero, philosopher, prolific writer of extended moral essays and moralizing letters addressed ostensibly to his friend Lucilius but intended for a wider audience, and the writer of the only tragic dramas that have survived intact from Latin literature, was a keen observer of the people and the world around him. The following passage from one of his letters to Lucilius gives a vivid impression of the sights and sounds at a private bathing establishment (**balneum**) in Rome. The translation below is adapted from that of Richard M. Gummere published in the Loeb Classical Library edition of Seneca and printed here with permission of Harvard University Press (all rights reserved).

Seneca, *Letters*, LVI.1–2

Nothing is more needed than silence for a man who secludes himself in order to study! Imagine what a variety of noises reverberates around my ears! I have lodgings right over a bathing establishment. So picture to yourself the assortment of sounds, which are strong enough to make me hate my very powers of hearing! When your strenuous gentleman, for example, is exercising himself by flourishing leaden weights; when he is working hard, or else pretends to be working hard, I can hear him grunt; and whenever he releases his imprisoned breath, I can hear him panting in wheezy and high-pitched tones. Or perhaps I notice some lazy fellow, content with a cheap rub-down, and hear the crack of the pummelling hand on his shoulder, varying in sound as the hand is laid on flat or hollow. Then, perhaps, a professional comes along, shouting out the score; that is the finishing touch. Add to this the arresting of a pickpocket, the racket of a man who always likes to hear his own voice in the bathroom, or the enthusiast who plunges into the swimming-tank with unconscionable noise and splashing. Besides all those whose voices, if nothing else, are good, imagine the hair-plucker with his penetrating, shrill voice—for purposes of advertisement—continually giving it vent and never holding his tongue except when he is plucking the armpits and making his victim yell instead. Then the cake-seller with his varied cries, the sausage-man, the confectioner, and all the vendors of food hawking their wares, each with his own distinctive intonation.

Pyramus and Thisbe

Publius Ovidius Naso (43 B.C.–A.D. 17), known today as Ovid, was one of Rome's greatest, most versatile, and most prolific poets. His epic poem of mythological tales, the *Metamorphoses*, written perhaps to rival the *Aeneid* of Vergil, has enjoyed immense popularity over the ages and has served as a source book for innumerable subsequent writers and artists. The story of Pyramus and Thisbe in Chapter 43 of the student's book is adapted from Book IV.55–166 of the *Metamorphoses*, and selections from Ovid's original Latin are given in Chapter 43 of the language activity book. The following translation of Ovid's version of the entire story is that of Rolfe Humphries (*Metamorphoses*, Indiana University Press, Bloomington, 1963) and is reprinted here with permission of the publisher (all rights reserved).

Ovid, *Metamorphoses* IV. 55–166

Next door to each other, in the brick-walled city
Built by Semiramis, lived a boy and girl,
Pyramus, a most handsome fellow, Thisbe,
Loveliest of all those Eastern girls. Their nearness
Made them acquainted, and love grew, in time,
So that they would have married, but their parents
Forbade it. But their parents could not keep them
From being in love: their nods and gestures
    showed it—
You know how fire suppressed burns all the
    fiercer.
There was a chink in the wall between the houses,
A flaw the careless builder never noticed,
Nor anyone else, for many years, detected,
But the lovers found it—love is a finder, always—
Used it to talk through, and the loving whispers
Went back and forth in safety. They would stand
One on each side, listening for each other,
Happy if each could hear the other's breathing,
And then they would scold the wall: "You envious
    barrier,
Why get in our way? Would it be too much to ask
    you
To open wide for an embrace, or even
Permit us room to kiss in? Still, we are grateful,
We owe you something, we admit; at least
You let us talk together." But their talking
Was futile, rather; and when evening came
They would say *Good night!* and give the good-
    night kisses
That never reached the other.

                    The next morning
Came, and the fires of night burnt out, and
    sunshine
Dried the night frost, and Pyramus and Thisbe
Met at the usual place, and first, in whispers,

47

Complained, and came—high time!—to a
  decision.
That night when all was quiet, they would fool
Their guardians, or try to, come outdoors,
Run away from home, and even leave the city.
And, not to miss each other, as they wandered
In the wide fields, where should they meet? At
  Ninus'
Tomb, they supposed was best; there was a tree
  there,
A mulberry-tree, loaded with snow-white berries,
Near a cool spring. The plan was good, the day-
  light
Was very slow in going, but at last
The sun went down into the waves, as always,
And the night rose, as always, from those waters.
And Thisbe opened her door, so sly, so cunning,
There was no creaking of the hinge, and no one
Saw her go through the darkness, and she came,
Veiled, to the tomb of Ninus, sat there waiting
Under the shadow of the mulberry-tree.
Love made her bold. But suddenly, here came
  something!—
A lioness, her jaws a crimson froth
With the blood of cows, fresh-slain, came there
  for water,
And far off through the moonlight Thisbe saw her
And ran, all scared, to hide herself in a cave,
And dropped her veil as she ran. The lioness
Having quenched her thirst, came back to the
  woods, and saw
The girl's light veil, and mangled it and mouthed
  it
With bloody jaws. Pyramus, coming there
Too late, saw tracks in the dust, turned pale, and
  paler
Seeing the bloody veil. "One night," he cried,
"Will kill two lovers, and one of them most surely,
Deserved a longer life. It is all my fault,
I am the murderer, poor girl; I told you
To come here in the night, to all this terror,
And was not here before you, to protect you.
Come, tear my flesh, devour my guilty body,
Come lions, all of you, whose lairs lie hidden
Under this rock! I am acting like a coward,
Praying for death." He lifts the veil and takes it
Into the shadow of their tree; he kisses
The veil he knows so well, his tears run down
Into its folds: "Drink my blood too!" he cries,
And draws his sword, and plunges it into his body,
And, dying, draws it out, warm from the wound.
As he lay there on the ground, the spouting blood
Leaped high, just as a pipe sends water spurting
Through a small hissing opening, when broken
With a flaw in the lead, and all the air is sprinkled.
The fruit of the tree, from that red spray, turned
  crimson,
And the roots, soaked with blood, dyed all the
  berries
The same dark hue.

Thisbe came out of hiding,
Still frightened, but a little fearful, also,
To disappoint her lover. She kept looking
Not only with her eyes, but all her heart,
Eager to tell him of those terrible dangers,
About her own escape. She recognized
The place, the shape of the tree, but there was
  something
Strange or peculiar in the berries' color.
Could this be right? And then she saw a quiver
Of limbs on bloody ground, and startled
  backward,
Paler than boxwood, shivering, as water
Stirs when a little breeze ruffles the surface.
It was not long before she knew her lover,
And tore her hair, and beat her innocent bosom
With her little fists, embraced the well-loved body,
Filling the wounds with tears and kissed the lips
Cold in his dying. "O my Pyramus,"
She wept, "What evil fortune takes you from me?
Pyramus, answer me! Your dearest Thisbe
Is calling you. Pyramus, listen! Lift your head!"
He heard the name of Thisbe, and he lifted
His eyes, with the weight of death heavy upon
  them,
And saw her face, and closed his eyes.

And Thisbe
Saw her own veil, and saw the ivory scabbard
With no sword in it, and understood. "Poor boy,"
She said, "So it was your own hand,
Your love, that took your life away. I too
Have a brave hand for this one thing, I too
Have love enough, and this will give me strength
For the last wound. I will follow you in death,
Be called the cause and comrade of your dying.
Death was the only one could keep you from me,
Death shall not keep you from me. Wretched
  parents
Of Pyramus and Thisbe, listen to us
Listen to both our prayers, do not begrudge us,
Whom death has joined, lying at last together
In the same tomb. And you, O tree, now shading
The body of one, and very soon to shadow
The bodies of two, keep in remembrance always
The sign of our death, the dark and mournful
  color."
She spoke, and fitting the sword-point at her
  breast,
Fell forward on the blade, still warm and reeking
With her lover's blood. Her prayers touched the
  gods
And touched her parents, for the mulberry fruit
Still reddens at its ripeness, and the ashes
Rest in a common urn.

Wild-Beast Hunts

The following extract from the *Scriptores Historiae
Augustae* may be read in conjunction with the note
titled "Other Shows in the Arena" on pages 58—59 of

the student's book. The passage concerns the Emperor Marcus Aurelius Probus (A.D. 232–282); the translation is that of David Magie published in the Loeb Classical Library edition of the *Scriptores Historiae Augustae* and printed here with permission of Harvard University Press (all rights reserved).

Scriptores Historiae Augustae, Probus, XIX-XX

Probus also gave the Romans their pleasures, and noted ones, too, and he bestowed largesses also. He celebrated a triumph over the Germans and the Blemmyae, and caused companies from all nations, each of them containing up to fifty men, to be led before his triumphal procession. He gave in the Circus a most magnificent wild-beast hunt, at which all things were to be the spoils of the people. Now the manner of this spectacle was as follows: great trees, torn up with the roots by the soldiers, were set up on a platform of beams of wide extent, on which earth was then thrown, and in this way the whole Circus, planted to look like a forest, seemed thanks to this new verdure, to be putting forth leaves. Then through all the entrances were brought in one thousand ostriches, one thousand stags and one thousand wild boars, then deer, ibexes, wild sheep, and other grass-eating beasts, as many as could be reared or captured. The populace was then let in, and each man seized what he wished. Another day he brought out in the Amphitheater, at a single performance one hundred maned lions, which woke the thunder with their roaring. All of these were slaughtered as they came out of the doors of their dens, and being killed in this way they afforded no great spectacle. For there was none of that rush on the part of the beasts which takes place when they are let loose from cages. Besides, many, unwilling to charge, were despatched with arrows. Then he brought out one hundred leopards from Libya, then one hundred from Syria, then one hundred lionesses and at the same time three hundred bears; all of which beasts, it is clear made a spectacle more vast than enjoyable. He presented besides, three hundred pairs of gladiators, among whom fought many of the Blemmyae, who had been led in his triumph, besides many Germans and Sarmatians also and even some Isaurian brigands.

Opposition to the Games

The following passage from Pliny's *Natural History* may be read in conjunction with the note titled "Opposition to the Games" on page 66 of the student's book, and also in conjunction with the passage from Cicero in Activity 48a of the language activity book. Compare Cicero's description of the compassion of the spectators for the elephants with the reaction of the audience to Pompey's elephants in Pliny's description which follows. The translation is that of H. Rackham published in the Loeb Classical Library edition of

Pliny's *Natural History* and printed here with permission of Harvard University Press (all rights reserved).

Pliny, Natural History, VIII. 19–22

Fenestella states that the first elephant fought in the Circus at Rome in the curule aedileship of Claudius Pulcher and the consulship of Marcus Antonius and Aulus Postumius, 99 B.C., and also that the first fight of an elephant against bulls was twenty years later in the curule aedileship of the Luculli. Also in Pompey's second consulship, at the dedication of the Temple of Venus Victrix, twenty, or, as some record, seventeen, fought in the Circus, their opponents being Gaetulians armed with javelins, one of the animals putting up a marvelous fight—its feet being disabled by wounds, it crawled against the hordes of the enemy on its knees, snatching their shields from them and throwing them into the air, and these as they fell delighted the spectators by the curves they described, as if they were being thrown by a skilled juggler and not by an infuriated wild animal. There was also a marvelous occurrence in the case of another, which was killed by a single blow, as the javelin striking it under the eye had reached the vital parts of the head. The whole band attempted to burst through the iron palisading by which they were enclosed and caused considerable trouble among the public. Owing to this, when subsequently Caesar in his dictatorship was going to exhibit a similar show he surrounded the arena with channels of water; these the emperor Nero removed when adding special places for the Knighthood. But Pompey's elephants when they had lost all hope of escape tried to gain the compassion of the crowd by indescribable gestures of entreaty, deploring their fate with a sort of wailing, so much to the distress of the public that they forgot the general and his munificence carefully devised for their honor, and bursting into tears rose in a body and invoked curses on the head of Pompey for which he soon afterwards paid the penalty. Elephants also fought for the dictator Caesar in his third consulship, twenty being matched against 500 foot soldiers, and on a second occasion an equal number carrying castles each with a garrison of 60 men, who fought a pitched battle against the same number of infantry as on the former occasion and an equal number of cavalry; and subsequently for the emperors Claudius and Nero elephants versus men single-handed, as the crowning exploit of the gladiators' careers.

St. Augustine (A.D. 354–430), the great Church Father who was thoroughly aware of the attractions of pagan culture, told the following story about a fellow-townsman and close associate of his whose strong and determined opposition to the games was overcome by one forced visit to the arena. The translation is that of John

K. Ryan published in *The Confessions of St. Augustine,* Image Books, Doubleday & Company, 1960, and is printed here with permission of the publisher (all rights reserved).

St. Augustine, *Confessions,* VI. 8

Since of course he did not plan to give up the worldly career that had been dinned into him by his parents, he had gone ahead of me to Rome to study law, and there he was carried off in an unbelievable way by the unbelievable passion for gladiatorial shows. Although he would have opposed such shows and detested them, certain of his friends and fellow students whom he chanced to meet as they were returning from dinner, in spite of the fact that he strongly objected and resisted them, dragged him with friendly force into the amphitheater on a day for these cruel and deadly games. All the while he was saying: "Even if you drag my body into this place, can you fasten my mind and eyes on such shows? I will be absent, though present, and thus I will overcome both them and you."

When they heard this, they nevertheless brought him in with them, perhaps wanting to find out if he would be able to carry it off. When they had entered and taken whatever places they could, the whole scene was ablaze with the most savage passions. He closed his eyes and forbade his mind to have any part in such evil sights. Would that he had been able to close his ears as well! For when one man fell in combat, a mighty roar went up from the entire crowd and struck him with such force that he was overcome by curiosity. As though he were well prepared to despise the sight and to overcome it, whatever it might be, he opened his eyes and was wounded more deeply in his soul than the man whom he desired to look at was in his body. He fell more miserably than did that gladiator at whose fall the shout was raised. The shout entered into him through his ears and opened up his eyes. The result was that there was wounded and struck down a spirit that was still bold rather than strong, and that was all the weaker because it presumed upon itself whereas it should have relied on you.

And he saw that blood, he drank in the savageness at the same time. He did not turn away, but fixed his sight on it, and drank in madness without knowing it. He took delight in that evil struggle, and he became drunk on blood and pleasure. He was no longer the man who entered there, but only one of the crowd that he had joined, and a true comrade of those who brought him there. What more shall I say? He looked, he shouted, he took fire, he bore away with himself a madness that should arouse him to return, not only with those who had drawn him there, but even before them, and dragging others along as well.

Centuries earlier than St. Augustine, Seneca had already warned of the dangers of mingling with the crowd and of how attendance at public spectacles can harm and corrupt a person. The following extract is from the same letter that is quoted on page 66 of the student's book. The translation is that of Richard M. Gummere published in the Loeb Classical Library edition of Seneca and is printed here with permission of Harvard University Press (all rights reserved).

Seneca, *Letters,* VII.1—3

Do you ask me what you should regard as especially to be avoided? I say, crowds; for as yet you cannot trust yourself to them with safety. I shall admit my own weakness, at any rate; for I never bring back home the same character I took abroad with me. Something of that which I have forced to be calm within me is disturbed; some of the foes I have routed return again. Just as the sick man, who has been weak for a long time, is in such a condition that he cannot be taken out of the house without suffering a relapse, so we ourselves are affected when our souls are recovering from a lingering disease. To consort with the crowd is harmful; there is no person who does not make some vice attractive to us, or stamp it upon us, or taint us unconsciously therewith. Certainly, the greater the mob with which we mingle, the greater the danger.

But nothing is so damaging to good character as the habit of lounging at the games; for then it is that vice steals subtly upon one through the avenue of pleasure. What do you think I mean? I mean that I come home more greedy, more ambitious, more voluptuous, and even more cruel and inhuman—because I have been among human beings.

Bridal Hymn

The following is a translation of the poem of Catullus from which **Versiculī** No. 29, "Bridal Hymn," on pages 122—123 of the student's book was taken. The bridegroom, Manlius Torquatus, may have been L. Manlius Torquatus, a younger contemporary of Catullus, who was praetor in 49 B.C. and served with Pompeian forces in Africa. Nothing more is known about his bride. The translation is that of Frank O. Copley published in *Gaius Valerius Catullus: The Complete Poetry,* The University of Michigan Press, 1966, and is printed here with permission of the publisher (all rights reserved).

Catullus, LXI

come from your hill, from Helicon,
come from your home, Urania's child
off to her husband steal the bride,
maid to her man, o wedding-god,
    O Hymen Hymenaeus

bind on your brow a flowered crown
of marjoram, the sweet-perfumed
put on the scarlet veil, be glad
glad as you come on snowy foot
    wearing the saffron sandal

come join us on our merry day
sing us the festal wedding-song
in little bell-tones high and clear
give us the beat to dance, lift up
    and swing the pine-torch blazing

here's Vinia, bride to Manlius,
(like Venus Idalian, on that day
she came before the Phrygian judge)
good virgin she, and good the signs
    that mark her day of marriage

call her a flower, call her bright
as any Asian myrtle-branch
that hamadryad elfin maids
plant in the garden where they play
    and nourish with the dew-drops

hither, then, Hymen, turn your steps
come, leave the land of Thespia,
the rock Aonian, and the cave
curtained by waters cool, where flow
    the streams of Aganippe.

summon the lady to house and home
for husband new her want awake
her heart with love bind all about
as ivy roving clings and folds
    the tree-trunk in its branches

and you too join us, pure and chaste
maids of honor (for you there comes
a day like this): take up the beat,
sing "Hymenaeus Hymen, O,
    O Hymen Hymenaeus"

gladden his heart when he shall hear
our prayer, for the task he loves
we bid him turn and come this way,
the guide of holy wedded love,
    the yoke of pure affection.

what god is more besought in prayer
by lovers loving and beloved?
to whom do men more honor pay
in heaven? O Hymen, wedding-god
    O Hymen Hymenaeus

"bless me and mine!" in quavering tones
some ancient prays; "for thee we loose
the virgin's knot," our maidens cry;
fearful of you but eager too
    the bridgroom waits your coming

into a young man's bold hot hands
the fragile bloom of a budding maid
you surrender, though still she clings
to mother's arms, O wedding-god
    O Hymen Hymenaeus.

without your blessing, love may take
no smallest profit that the world
would count as lawful, but it may
with your consent: who to this god
    would dare declare him equal?

without your blessing there's no house
can bring forth children, there's no sire
can hope for offspring, but they can
with your consent: who to this god
    would dare declare him equal?

the land that knew naught of your rites
could never bring forth guardians
to watch its boundaries, but it could
with your consent: who to this god
    would dare declare him equal?

draw back the bolts! fling wide the doors!
here comes the bride! the torches, see,
how shine and shimmer their fiery locks!
. . . .
   . . . .

her maiden modesty slows her step
. . . .
to this she yet gives readier ear
. . . .
    she weeps that it's time to be going.

come, dry your tears! you run no risk,
Aurunculeia, that on the morn
some woman lovelier than you
may see the dawn send up its beams
    bright from the eastern Ocean

like you, in a rich lord's garden plot,
'mid all the colors massed and bright
stands out the bloom of the fleur-de-lis
but you're delaying: the hour is late
    come out, new bride, to your wedding!

come out, new bride, to your wedding now,
come, if you please, come out and hear
the song we sing: the torches, see,
how golden shimmering shine their locks
    come out, new bride, to your wedding

your husband, long as you both shall live,
will keep him only unto you
he'll do no wrong, no shameful thing
nor look to lie in other beds
    apart from your young body

no, rather, as the clinging vine
enfolds the tree that grows nearby
he will be close within your arms
enfolded—but the hour is late
    come out, new bride, to your wedding

o, marriage bed, that to all men
. . . .
   . . . .
     . . . .
    a bed's foot white and shining

what great delights are on their way
to your young master while the hours
of night speed by; what joys he'll know
at mid-day—but the hour is late
   come out, new bride, to your wedding

lift up your torches, boys, I see
the scarlet veil is on the way
come, take up the beat, together sing
"O Hymenaeus Hymen, O
   O Hymen Hymenaeus!"

           ***

we know that you have only known
what is lawful—but you're married now
and what is lawful's not the same
O Hymenaeus Hymen O
   O Hymen Hymenaeus

and you, too, bride, take care: don't say
"no" to what your husband will ask
or he'll go asking otherwhere
O Hymen Hymenaeus O
   O Hymen Hymenaeus

look, bride: the house! your husband's house!
how rich and powerful it is
say but the word, 'twill be your slave
(O Hymen Hymenaeus O
   O Hymen Hymenaeus)

until the day when old age comes
and palsy makes your hoary head
nod "yes" to all, to everything
O Hymen Hymenaeus O
   O Hymen Hymenaeus

lift up (good luck! don't stumble here!)
across the threshold your golden feet
pass through the shining doorway smooth
O Hymen Hymenaeus O
   O Hymen Hymenaeus

see there! within the house he lies,
your husband, on his Tyrian couch
waiting and watching all for you
O Hymen Hymenaeus O
   O Hymen Hymenaeus

for him no lower than for you
flickers within his heart of hearts
the flame, but deeper down it lies
O Hymen Hymenaeus O
   O Hymen Hymenaeus

let go the lovely rounded arm
of our sweet maid, young acolyte
up to the bride-bed let her come
O Hymen Hymenaeus O
   O Hymen Hymenaeus

and you, good matrons, whom your men
have loved so well for years and years,
come, lay our sweet maid in her bed
O Hymen Hymenaeus O
   O Hymen Hymenaeus

now, husband, come: it is your time
your wife lies in the bridal room
see how there shines upon her face
the white bloom of the maiden-flower
   the red glow of the poppy

but, husband, by the powers above,
you're no less handsome than your bride
our Lady Venus never thought
to scorn you—but the hour is late
   come on now, don't be lagging

ah, there you are! you haven't lagged
for long. may Holy Venus shed
a blessing on you, since your want
is honest want, and since your love
   is unconcealed and lawful.

who'd count the sands of Africa?
who'd number all the twinkling stars?
a man would sooner reckon up
their totals than he'd know the tale
   of times you'll sport together.

sport as you will, and may you soon
be blessed with children: it's not right
that any name as old as yours
should fail of children: let it be
   of offspring ever fertile

a tiny Torquatus I'd like to see
safe in his mother's circling arms
hold out his darling baby hands
and give his father that first fleet smile
   with little lips half-parted

may he reflect his father's face:
a Manlius beyond all doubt
known on the spot by everyone;
and, for his mother, may he show
   her virtue by his features

and may he prove his mother's son
in goodness that will gain him praise
just as men called Telemachus
"the Good" and in his goodness saw
   Penelope, his mother

come, maids of honor, close the door
we've had our fun. Husband and wife,
we wish you every happiness
may health and youth and love and life
   bring you delights unending.

Roman Funerals

The following account by Vergil of the funeral of Misenus may be compared with the description of Roman
funerals on page 103 of the student's book and with
the funeral of Titus described in the story in Chapter
53. Although set in the heroic age, the funeral of
Misenus follows the rituals used in funerals of Vergil's
times. The details are vividly narrated. The translation
is that of Frank O. Copley published in *The Aeneid, The*

Vergil, *Aeneid*, VI. 162–3, 175–84, 212–35

But high on the beach as they came in they found
Misenus, untimely taken off by death—

***

Now, circling round, the company mourned his
   death,
Aeneas leading. Then, with tears, they turned
to the Sibyl's orders. Quickly they built a mound
and altar, and piled on logs to reach the sky.
They went to a wood, the wild beasts' mountain
   lair:
down came the pine, the oak rang to the axe,
the beech and holm were hewn and split to rail
and billet; great elms came rolling from the hills.
In this work, too, Aeneas took the lead,
urged on his men, and shared their tools and toil.

***

Meanwhile down on the shore the Trojans
   mourned
Misenus in thankless office for the dead.
They built his pyre with pitch pine and split oak,
like one great torch, and then with dull dark
   leaves
they screened its sides. In front they set the
   cypress,
the death tree; shining armor graced the top.
Some set bronze pots of water over flame
to boil, then washed the body and embalmed it.
They wailed the dead, then laid him on the bier,
and covered him with the purple robe he'd known
and loved. They lifted high his heavy bed—
sad office—and in our fathers' way applied
the torch with face averted. Up went the pyre:
incense, food, and oil and wine commingled.
When cinders crumbled and the flames died
   down,
they quenched the dust and thirsty ash with wine.
Corynaeus gathered the bones in a brazen urn;
he bore pure water three times round his friends,
sprinkling them with hyssop of fertile olive,
to wash them clean, then said the last farewell.
Aeneas the good piled high a mounded tomb
(placing upon it the man's arms, oar, and trumpet)
beneath the crag that men now call, for him,
"Mount Misenus," to keep his name forever.

Bibliography and Useful Information for Teachers

I. BOOKS AND ARTICLES REFERRED TO IN THE TEACHER'S HANDBOOK

Note that references have usually been restricted to books that are currently in print. Many other resources can be found in libraries. Asterisks in the list below mark books regarded as highly recommended for the school library. Double asterisks mark books that should be available as basic resources in the Latin classroom.

Ancient Rome, by Nicholas Sherwin-White. "Then and There Series," Longman, New York, 1978. 96 pp., illustrated, paperback. A brief account for junior and senior high school students.

***Aspects of Roman Life Folder A*. Longman, New York, 1975. Contains 32 yellow source sheets, 4 sheets of photos, 1 sheet of plans, 2 sheets of models, and 8 double-sided work cards on 16 different topics (4 copies of each work card per set of materials). To accompany the booklets titled *Roman Towns*, *The Roman House*, and *Roman Family Life* in the Longman "Aspects of Roman Life" series. Suitable for late elementary grades and junior high school.

***City: A Story of Roman Planning and Construction*, by David Macaulay. Houghton Mifflin Company, Boston, MA, 1974. 112 pp., illustrated. The layout and building of an imaginary Roman town in northern Italy. Captivating illustrations. For all ages.

**Daily Life in Ancient Rome; The People and the City at the Height of the Empire*, by Jerome Carcopino, edited by Henry T. Rowell, translated by E. O. Lorimer. Yale University Press, New Haven, CT, 1940. xi + 342 pp., paperback. A detailed study of Roman life; background for the teacher and an excellent resource for students' projects.

Death and Burial in the Roman World, by J.M.C. Toynbee. "Aspects of Greek and Roman Life" series. Cornell University Press, Ithaca, NY, 1971. 336 pp., illustrated. An excellent reference work for high school students and teachers and a useful resource book for students' projects.

Gladiators, by Michael Grant. (out of print).

Goddesses, Whores, Wives, and Slaves: Women in Classical Antiquity, by Sarah B. Pomeroy. Schocken Books, New York, 1975. xiii + 265 pp., illustrated, paperback. Of special interest is Chapter VIII, "The Roman Matron of the Late Republic and Early Empire"; background for the teacher.

Imperial Rome, by Moses Hadas. Time-Life Books, Alexandria, VA.

Pictorial Dictionary of Ancient Rome, by Ernest Nash. Frederick A. Praeger: now distributed by Hacker Art Books, NY, 1961, (2nd ed., revised). Volume I, 544 pp., Volume II, 535 pp., both lavishly illustrated. An authoritative pictorial survey of the monuments and ruins of ancient Rome, arranged alphabetically. Extremely useful.

Roman Architecture, by Frank Brown. "The Great Ages of World Architecture" series. George Braziller, New York, 1982. 125 pp., illustrated, paperback. Informative, incisive text; excellent illustrations; primarily background for the teacher.

Roman Architecture, by Frank Sear. Cornell University Press, Ithaca, NY, 1983.

Roman Art and Architecture, by Mortimer Wheeler. "World of Art" series. Oxford University Press, New York and Toronto, 1964. 250 pp., illustrated, many in color, paperback. A general survey with good illustrations; for high school students and teachers.

Roman Civilization Sourcebook II: The Empire, by Naphtali Lewis and Meyer Reinhold. "Harper Torchbooks" edition. Harper & Row, New York, 1966. viii + 652 pp., paperback. Passages from ancient authors and documents in English translation. An excellent reference work for the teacher and a useful resource book for students' projects.

Roman Family Life, by Peter Hodge, "Aspects of Roman Life" series. Longman, New York, 1974. 62 pp., illustrated, paperback. A student's textbook for study of Roman culture; contains discussions of various topics, quotations of ancient sources, illustrations, study questions, and suggestions for projects. Suitable for late elementary and junior high school.

Roman Life, by Mary Johnston. Scott, Foresman and Company, Glenview, IL, 1957. 478 pp., illustrated. Very informative; excellent reference work for high school students and teachers. A useful resource book for students' projects.

Roman Religion, by Michael Massey. "Aspects of Roman Life" series. Longman, White Plains, NY, 1979. 48 pp., illustrated, paperback. Same comments apply as to *Roman Family Life* above.

Roman Sport and Entertainment, by David Buchanan. "Aspects of Roman Life" series. Longman, New York, 1975. 62 pp., illustrated, paperback. Same comments apply as to *Roman Family Life* above.

Roman Towns, by Peter Hodge. "Aspects of Roman Life" series. Longman, New York, 1977. 48 pp., illustrated, paperback. Same comments apply as to *Roman Family Life* above.

Rome and Environs, edited by Alta Macadam. "Blue Guide" series. W. W. Norton, New York, 1979 (2nd ed.). 402 pp., plus maps, illustrated, paperback. A detailed and authoritative guide to the city and its environs with an emphasis on the ancient monuments.

Rome: Its People, Life and Customs, by Ugo Enrico Paoli, translated by R.D. Macnaghten. Longman, New York, 1963. xiii + 336 pp., illustrated. Excellent, detailed, well-documented accounts of all major aspects of Roman culture. A basic background book for students and teachers to use in conjunction with ECCE ROMANI. Suitable for high school students and teachers.

Spartacus, by Howard Fast. Dell, New York, 1980; Buccaneer Books, Cutchogue, NY, 1982; G. K. Hall & Co., Boston, 1984.

The Colosseum, by Peter Quennell. (out of print) "Wonders of Man" series. Newsweek, New York, 1971.

The Emperor Titus: A Reassessment, by B. W. Jones. St. Martin's Press, New York, 1984. 272 pp. A biography of the Emperor; background for the teacher.

The Languages of the World, by Kenneth Katzner. Funk & Wagnalls, New York, 1975. x + 374 pp., tables. A 38-page discussion of language family-groups, followed by an extensive presentation of literary samples of 200 languages, translated and discussed, and ending with a country-by-country survey of the languges in present use. A most useful and interesting reference book for both student and teacher.

The Mute Stones Speak: The Story of Archaeology in Italy, by Paul MacKendrick. Norton, New York, 1983 (2nd ed.). xix + 491 pp., illustrated, paperback. A general survey suitable for high school students and teachers.

The Oxford Classical Dictionary, ed. by N. G. L. Hammond and H. H. Scullard. Oxford University Press, New York, 1970 (2nd ed.). xxii + 1176 pp. Detailed, scholarly background material for the teacher.

The Story of Language, by Mario Pei. The New American Library, New York, 1965. 508 pp., paperback. A most readable general study of the languages of the world, past and present, containing a wealth of information on the forces affecting the development, modification, and decline of languages. Suitable for mature high school students and teachers.

The Story of Latin and the Romance Languages, by Mario Pei. Harper & Row, 1976. xx + 356 pp., maps. Comprehensive study of the historical, geographical, and psychological factors in the development of the

Romance languages from Latin, beginning with a survey of historical background from the ancient Romans to the rise of the Romance nations, followed by a detailed study of the ancient languages of Italy, the development and flowering of Latin, and the evolution of the Romance tongues. For able high school students and teachers.

Women's Life in Greece & Rome: A Source Book in Translation, by Mary R. Lefkowitz and Maureen B. Fant. The Johns Hopkins University Press, Baltimore, MD, 1982. xvi + 294 pp., paperback. A well-organized selection of passages on a wide variety of topics; excellent reference book.

II. GENERAL BOOKS ON ANCIENT ROME AND ITS CULTURE AND CIVILIZATION

The Ancient Romans, by Chester G. Starr. Oxford University Press, NY, 1971. Illustrated, paperback. A comprehensive treatment.

The Civilization of Rome, by Donald R. Dudley. "A Mentor Book." The New American Library, New York, 1962. 256 pp., illustrated, paperback. An account for teachers and mature high school students.

The Romans, by R. H. Barrow. Penguin Books, New York, 1975. 223 pp. A fairly broad, general account of the character of the Romans and their achievements.

The Romans: An Introduction to Their History and Civilization, by Karl Christ. University of California Press, Berkeley, CA, 1984. 275 pp. A detailed, authoritative historical and cultural survey of the Romans.

The Romans and Their World, by Peter D. Arnott. St. Martin's Press, New York, 1970. 318 pp., illustrated, paperback. Interesting background reading for the teacher and mature high school students.

III. BACKGROUND BOOKS FOR WORD STUDY

*English Words from Latin and Greek Elements, by Donald M. Ayers. University of Arizona Press, Tucson, AZ, 1986 (2nd ed.). xx + 290 pp., paperback. A useful "Introduction" on the Indo-European family of languages and the background of English vocabulary is followed by chapters introducing prefixes, suffixes, and bases and discussing various linguistic phenomena that have shaped the English language. Highly recommended as background for the teacher.

Latin and Greek in Current Use, Eli E. Burriss and Lionel Casson. Prentice-Hall, Englewood Cliffs, NJ, 1949. xi + 292 pp. An alternative to the book listed above.

*Latin-English Derivative Dictionary, by Rudolf F. Schaeffer. American Classical League, Miami University, Oxford, OH, 1960. 48 pp., paperback. A useful dictionary listing the English derivatives from Latin words.

*Latin Words in Current English, by Graydon W. Regenos. American Classical League, Miami University, Oxford, OH. 54 pp., paperback. Over 7,000 words that have come into English from Latin with few or no changes.

The Romance Languages: A Linguistic Introduction, by Rebecca Posner. Peter Smith, Gloucester, MA, 1970, reprint of Doubleday Anchor Books Edition, 1966. xix + 336 pp., maps. Scholarly study of the development of the vocabulary, grammar, and sounds of Romance languages from their roots in Latin. Specialized background for the teacher.

Word Ancestry: Interesting Stories of the Origins of English Words, by Willis A. Ellis. American Classical League, Miami University, Oxford, OH. 62 pp., paperback. Stories of English words, most of them derived from Greek or Latin.

IV. POSTERS AND MAPS

**"Map of Rome." Line drawing of ancient Rome. 19" × 13", identifying the most important sites and structures of the city of Rome during the Republican and Imperial eras. American Classical League, Miami University, Oxford, OH 45056. (Order Number P101)

For other maps available, consult the surveys of audiovisual materials published in *The Classical World* (see section VI of this Bibliography).

V. LATIN LANGUAGE BOOKS

Allen and Greenough's New Latin Grammar for Schools and Colleges, edited by J. B. Greenough, G. L. Kittredge, A. A. Howard, and Benjamin L. D'Ooge. Caratzas Brothers, New Rochelle, NY, 1975. 490 pp., paperback.

Cassell's New Compact Latin Dictionary. Dell Distributing, New York, 1981. 384 pp., paperback.

Cassell's Latin Dictionary, Latin-English, English-Latin, edited by D. P. Simpson. Macmillan Co., New York, 1977.

Latin: A Historical and Linguistic Handbook, by Mason Hammond. Harvard University Press, Cambridge, MA, 1976. ix + 292 pp., paperback. A useful historical and linguistic introduction to Latin written with high school Latin teachers in mind.

Latin Word Lists: Years One Through Four with English Meanings and Instructions in Latin Word Formation, by John K. Colby. Independent School Press, Wellesley Hills, MA, 1978. 47 pp., paperback. Standard listing of words to be mastered in the first four levels of Latin.

New College Latin and English Dictionary, by John C. Traupman. Amsco School Publications, New York, 1966, and Bantam Books, New York, 1970.

**Orbis Pictus Latinus: Illustrated Latin Dictionary*, by Hermann Koller. Longman, New York, 1983. 431 pp., illustrated, paperback. An intriguing dictionary with simple Latin definitions of interesting, culture-laden Latin words.

Oxford Latin Dictionary, edited by P. G. W. Glare. Oxford University Press, New York, 1983. xxiv + 2,126 pp. The definitive Latin dictionary for schools and colleges.

VI. ANCIENT AND MODERN PRIMARY SOURCES

Roman Voices: Everyday Latin in Ancient Rome, by Carol Clemeau Esler. Available from Gilbert Lawall, 71 Sand Hill Road, Amherst, MA 01002. 1982, 161 pp., paperback.

Teacher's Guide to Roman Voices, by Carol Clemeau Esler. Available as above. 1984, 62 pp., paperback. A translation key for the book above; also contains additional non-literary and literary Latin texts.

Ancient authors have usually been quoted in the cultural readings in the student's book and in most of the quotations in the teacher's handbook from the translations in the Loeb Classical Library series, usually with some adaptations. These translations are published with permission of Harvard University Press (all rights reserved). The following list of authors and works in the Loeb Classical Library series is provided for reference (each volume contains the Latin text and facing translation, plus introduction and notes). The list is alphabetical by name of the author.

Livy, tr. B. O. Foster
Ovid: Fasti, tr. Sir J. G. Frazer
Pliny: Natural History, tr. H. Rackham
Scriptores Historiae Augustae, tr. David Magie
Seneca: Epistulae Morales, tr. R. M. Gummere
Suetonius, tr. J. C. Rolfe
Virgil, tr. H. Rushton Fairclough

Translations from the following also appear in the cultural background readings at the end of the teacher's handbook:

Catullus: *Catullus: The Complete Poetry*, tr. Frank O. Copley, The Unversity of Michigan Press, Ann Arbor, MI, 1957.

Ovid: *Metamorphoses*, tr. Rolfe Humphries, Indiana University Press, Bloomington, 1963.

St. Augustine: *The Confessions of St. Augustine*, tr. John K. Ryan, Doubleday & Co., Garden City, NY, 1960.

Vergil: *Vergil: The Aeneid*, tr. Frank O. Copley, The Bobbs-Merrill Company, New York, 1965.

Principal Parts of Verbs

Following is a list of verbs of which the principal parts are given in the designated chapters (for the purposes of this list, see page 52 of the second teacher's handbook).

47	admīror	43	exprimō	43	occīdō
41	admittō	42	exsiliō	53	operiō
51	agō	53	exstruō	46	ostendō
50	amplector	41	exuō	47	parcō
52	ardeō	53	frangō	43	perdō
43	aspergō	49	grātulor	50	praecipiō
41	cognōscō	53	hortor	42	prehendō
47	cōgō	48	immittō	51	prōferō
50	comitor	46	incēdō	53	quiēscō
53	compōnō	48	incipiō	41	repetō
41	concrepō	53	ingravēscō	43	sentiō
42	cōnfugiō	48	intellegō	49	spondeō
46	cōnsistō	52	iungō	42	subsequor
50	conticēscō	42	lābor	42	surripiō
46	convertō	44	laedō	41	tergeō
41	corrumpō	47	lambō	46	tollō
53	dēcēdō	53	linquō	41	unguō
41	dēfricō	45	mālō	51	urgeō
49	dēspondeō	48	mīror	43	valedīcō
53	dīligō	49	neglegō	47	vescor
53	eximō	52	nūbō	43	vīvō

LATIN VOCABULARIES CHAPTERS 41 to 43

NOUNS

calor	ōsculum	*turba
*cōnsilium	pavīmentum	vapor
*digitus	rīma	vēlāmen
follis	*scelus	*vestibulum
*fūr	*senātus	*vestīmenta
*lacrima	senex	*virgō
*leō	spēlunca	*vultus

ADJECTIVES

calvus	*rīdiculus
capillātus	*saevus
*commūnis	sanguineus
īnscius	*uterque
*prior	varius

VERBS

*admittere	*occīdere
aspergere	perdere
*cognōscere	*prehendere
concrepāre	*prōcēdere
cōnfugere	repetere
convenīre	rīxārī
corrumpere	*sentīre
dēfricāre	*subsequī
*exercere	*surripere
exprimere	tergere
exsilīre	unguere
exuere	*valedīcere
*lābī	*vīvere

MISCELLANEOUS

cōnsilium capere	*nec
*forte	*noctū
*haud	*posteā
*haud multō post	*prope (adv.)
*humī	sēcrētō

LATIN VOCABULARIES CHAPTERS 44 to 48

NOUNS

bēstiārius	*gladiātor	*mūnera
cavea	*impetus	*peristȳlium
crūdēlitās	*lūdus	pūpa
*fēmina	*magistrātus	stirps
*furor	*merīdiēs	tigris

ADJECTIVES

ambō	*mīrābilis
claudus	*mītis
*immānis	*negōtiōsus
mānsuētus	obstupefactus
memorābilis	reservātus

VERBS

*admīrārī	immittere	*mālle
*circumspicere	incēdere	*mīrārī
*cōgere	*incipere	*ostendere
condemnāre	*intellegere	*parcere
congredī	introdūcere	*putāre
*cōnsistere	*laedere	*referre
*cōnstat	lambere	*spērāre
convertere	*latēre	*tollere
ēdūcere	*līberāre	vescī

PREPOSITIONS

*contrā

MISCELLANEOUS

*ācriter	metū exanimātus
admīrātiōnī esse	nōbīs redeundum est
admīrātiōne captus	*Num . . .?
aliās	omnium cōnsēnsū
amor ac dēliciae generis hūmānī	placidē
bonō animō es (este)	*postrēmō
clāmātum est	*prius
clēmenter et blandē	*prō certō habeō
*diēs nātālis	pugnam committere
dōnō dare	*quasi
epistula est cōnficienda	Quid Sextō fīet?
*ferē	quō maior . . eō plūs
mātūrē	*rē vērā
*māvult	*tot

LATIN VOCABULARIES CHAPTERS 49 to 53

NOUNS

ānulus	fūnus	myrtus
*āra	*gēns	*nātus (gnātus)
auspex	hilaritās	*patrēs
*avis	incessus	prōnuba
*benevolentia	*ingenium	prūdentia
caterva	*iuvenis	*pulchritūdō
*cognōmen	Larēs	*sacra
cōnsultum	laurus	*sermō
*cor	*līberta	*serva
coxa	*līmen	*sōl
*dextra	*marītus	*sōlitūdō
epulae	*mātrōna	*spōnsa
*familia	medicus	*spōnsus
*familiārēs	*monumentum	viscera
febris	*morbus	*vīta
*fidēs	*mōs	vitta

VERBS

ait	*frangere	*optāre
amplectī	grātulārī	*ōrāre
aptāre	*hortārī	*ornāre
*ardēre	*imperāre	perferre
āvertere	impōnere	perlegere
comitārī	*incidere	*praebēre
*commemorāre	ingravēscere	*praecēdere
compōnere	inicere	*praecipere
conticēscere	*interrogāre	prōferre
dēcēdere	introīre	prōrumpere
dēdūcere	*iungere	*quiēscere
*dēspondēre	*linquere	recipere
*dīligere	*locāre	rescrībere
ēnuntiāre	*neglegere	*sacrificāre
excēdere	*nūbere	*spondēre
eximere	*observāre	urgēre
*exstruere	operīre	*violāre

ADJECTIVES

*albus	nōnnūllī
*cārus	perturbātus
castus	*posterus
*commodus	*postrēmus
conversus	praetextātus
dēditus	*propīnquus
eximius	*pūblicus
*familiāris	*puerīlis
*fūnebris	sēdecim
hilaris	serēnus
lepidus	siccus
*levis	*similis
lūbricus	*sinister
*nōbilis	trepidāns

PREPOSITIONS

ergā

MISCELLANEOUS

*adeō	merita cōnferre
*cum	mortiferē
cūrae esse	nē quis
Dīs Mānibus	*nōn decet patrem
eō magis	*nova nūpta
erat īnscrībendum	nūper
est arcessendus	*paulō post
exsequiās dūcere	*placuit
*grātiās agere	*potius . . . quam
Heus!	rīte
*honōris causā	sī quis
id quod	*tē oportet
*in mātrimōnium dūcere	*utrum . . . an
*mē taedet	

ENGLISH-LATIN VOCABULARY

Vocabulary for Activities 41e, RXa, 44d, 45c, 46d, RXIa, 49e, 49f, 50d, and RXIIa

a

able: **posse**
above: **suprā**
actually: **rē vērā**
advance: **prōgredī**
afraid: **timēre** or **verērī**
after: consider using ablative
  absolute
again: **iterum**
agree (it is agreed): **cōnstat**
all: **omnis**
alone: **sōlus**
also: **quoque**
among: **inter** (+ *acc.*)
amphitheater: **amphitheātrum**
ancient: **vetus**
and they: use linking **quī**
and: **et** or **-que**
angry: **īrātus**
animals: **pecora**
approach: **prōcēdere** (+ **ad** + *acc.*)
arrive at: **pervenīre** (+ **ad** + *acc.*)
as if: **tamquam**
as: **ut** (+ *indicative*)
ask: **rogāre**
attack: **adorīrī**
attend: **ministrāre**

b

bag: **follis**
bald: **calvus**
ball: **pila**
bathe: **sē lavāre**
baths: **thermae**
be: **esse**
beautiful: **pulcher**
become: **fierī**
began: **coepisse**
believe: **crēdere**
between: **inter** (+ *acc.*)
boy: **puer**
bride's attendant: **prōnuba**
bride: **spōnsa**
build: **aedificāre**
but: **sed**
buy: **emere**
by: **ā** or **ab** (+ *abl.*)
bystanders: **adstantēs**

c

celebrate: **celebrāre**
certain: **certus**
changing room: **apodytērium**
chess: **latrunculī**
children: **līberī**
citizen: **cīvis**
city: **urbs**
clothed: **indūtus**
clothes: **vestīmenta** or **vestēs**
come (to): **adīre**

come: **venīre**
commonly: **plērumque**
concerning: **dē** (+ *abl.*)
connect: **connectere**
consult: **cōnsulere**
couch: **lectus**

d

daughter: **fīlia**
dead: **mortuus**
death: **mors**
decide: **cōnstituere**
delight: **dēlectāre**
demand: **poscere**
descend: **dēscendere**
diligently (very): **dīligentissimē**
discover: **repperīre**
do: **facere**
doll: **pūpa**
drag: **trahere**
dress in: **induere** + *abl.*
drink: **sūmere**

e

Egypt: **Aegyptus**
emperor: **prīnceps**
empire: **imperium**
enter: **intrāre** or **ingredī**
entrance passage: **vestibulum**
even: **etiam**
ever: **umquam**
every: **omnis**
everyone: **omnēs**
exercise ground: **palaestra**
exhausted: **dēfessus**
extend: **pergere**

f

fall: **cadere**
farm: **vīlla rūstica**
farmhouse: **vīlla**
father: **pater**
fear: **metus**
fee: **pecūnia**
finally: **tandem**
find out: **cognōscere**
find: **invenīre**
finger: **digitus**
for a long time: **diū**
for: **nam**
friend: **amīcus** or **amīca**
friendly (in a friendly way):
  cōmiter
frighten: **terrēre**
frightened: **perterritus**
from: **ā** or **ab** (+ *abl.*)
from: **dē** (+ *abl.*)
full: **plēnus** (+ *abl.*)

g

games: **lūdī**
give back: **reddere**

give: **dare**
go into: **inīre**
go to sleep: **obdormīre**
go: **īre** or **venīre**
god: **deus**
golden: **aureus**
Greek: **Graecus**
groan: **gemere**
groom: **spōnsus**
ground: **terra**
guard: **custōs**

h

hair (with long): **capillātus**
hand over: **trādere**
hand: **manus**
happen: **fierī** or **accidere**
happy: **laetus** or **beātus**
have: **habēre**
head: **caput**
hear: **audīre**
heart: **cor**
him: **eum**
himself: **sē**
his: **eius**
hold: **tenēre**
house: **vīlla**
how: **quōmodo**

i

I: **ego**
if: **sī**
immediately: **statim**
in a friendly way: **cōmiter**
in honor of: use *dat.*
in this way: **ita** or **sīc**
in: after "clothed," use *abl.*
in: **in** (+ *abl.*)
into: **in** (+ *acc.*)
invite: **invītāre** or **vocāre**
it: **is**

k

kill: **necāre**
king: **rēx**
kiss: **ōsculum**
know: **scīre**

l

lead: **dūcere**
left (the left): **laeva**
left: **sinister**
lie: **recumbere**
life: **vīta**
long (with long hair): **capillātus**
long-haired: **capillātus**
loudly: **magnā vōce**

m

magnificent: **magnificus**
make: **facere**
man: **homō**
many: **multī**

master: **dominus**
may: **licet** + *dat.* and *infinitive*
me (*dat.*): **mihi**
me (*acc.*): **mē**
messenger: **nūntius**
mind: **animus**
mother: **māter**
multitude: **multitūdō**
must: **oportet** + *acc.* and *infinitive*
my: **meus**

n
nearest: **proximus**
neighboring: **vīcīnus**
nerve: **nervus**
never: **numquam**
night: **nox**
no: **nūllus**
nose: **nāsus**
not know: **nescīre**
not wish: **nōlle**
not: **nōn**

o
often: **saepe**
old man: **senex**
on: **ad** (+ *acc.*)
on: **in** (+ *abl.*)
once upon a time: **ōlim**
onto: **in** (+ *acc.*)
opportunity: **occāsiō**
opposite: **contrā**
order: **iubēre**
other: **alius**

p
part: **pars**
pay (a fee): **dare**
people: **populus**
perfume: **unguentum**
pick up: **repetere** or **tollere**
place: **locus**
play: **lūdere**
please: **placet** + *dat.* and *infinitive*
praise: **laudāre**
prefer: **mālle**
prepare: **parāre**

q
quickly: **celeriter**
quietly: **placidē**

r
receive: **accipere**
red: **russātus**
remain: **manēre**
rest: **quiēscere**
return: **regredī**
ridiculous: **rīdiculōsus**
right hand: **dextra**
ring: **ānulus**
run (this way and that): **concursāre**
run into: **incurrere**
run: **currere**

s
say: **dīcere**
say: **inquit**
see: **vidēre**
seem: **vidērī**
seize: **prehendere**
send: **mittere**
shortage: **penūria**
should: **decet** + *acc.* and *infinitive*
shout: **clāmāre**
sign: **signum**
signal: **signum**
since: consider using a future active participle
since: **cum** (+ *subjunctive*)
sit down: **cōnsīdere**
sit: **sedēre**
sky: **caelum**
slave: **servus**
sleep (go to sleep): **obdormīre**
smallest: **minimus**
snap (fingers): **concrepāre**
snatch: **arripere**
so: **tam**
soon: **brevī tempore**
soul: **anima**
spectacule: **spectāculum**
spectator: **spectātor**
stand nearby: **adstāre**
stand: **stāre**
steal: **surripere**
stick: **baculum**
stone: **lapis**
suddenly: **subitō**
suspend: **dēmittere**
sword: **gladius**

t
take off: **exuere**
take: **capere**
taste: **dēgustāre**
tell: **dīcere**
that: **is**
that: **quī**
that: **ut** (+ *subjunctive*)
them: **eae**
then: **deinde** or **tum**
therefore: **propterea**
thief: **fūr** or **praedō**
thin: **tenuis**
thing: **rēs**
think: **putāre** or **crēdere**
this way and that: **hūc illūc**
this: **hic**
time: **tempus**
tired of: **taedet** + *acc.* and *gen.*
to be: **esse**, but sometimes not translated
to: **ad** (+ *acc.*)
tombstone: **stēla**
tomorrow: **crās**

toward: **ad** (+ *acc.*)
try: **cōnārī**
tunic: **tunica**
two: **duo**
tyrant: **tyrannus**

u
understand: **intellegere**
unreasonable: **īnscītus**
urge: **hortārī**
us: **nōs**

v
very diligently: **dīligentissimē**
very many: **plūrimī**
visit: **vīsitāre**

w
walk: **ambulāre**
want: **cupere**
warm: **calidus**
watch: **spectāre**
way (in this way): **ita** or **sic**
way (this way and that): **hūc illūc**
wear: **ūsitārī** + *abl.*
wedding: **nūptiae**
What . . .?: **Quid . . .?**
what: **quid**
when: consider using participle
when: consider using ablative absolute
when: **cum** (+ *subjunctive*)
where: **ubi**
which: **quī**
who: consider using perfect participle
who: **quī**
why: **cūr**
wicked: **scelestus**
wife: **uxor**
win: **vincere**
wine: **vīnum**
wish: **cupere** or **velle**
with long hair: **capillātus**
with me: **mēcum**
with: consider using ablative absolute
with: **cum** (+ *abl.*)
without: **sine** (+ *abl.*)
wolf: **lupus**
woman: **fēmina** or **mulier**
wonder: **mīrārī**
worried: **sollicitus**

y
you: **tū**

Syntax

I. NOUNS

A. Dative Case

1. Two datives may be used together in what is called the *double dative* construction. One of the datives is a *dative of reference*, denoting the person or thing concerned, and the other is a *dative of purpose*:

> **Omnēs spectātōribus admīrātiōnī fuērunt leōnēs. . . .** (47:1–2)
> Literally, *All the lions were for the purpose of wonder with reference to the spectators*, better English, *All the lions were a source of wonder to the spectators.*

2. The dative is used with certain adjectives (*dative with special adjectives*):

> **Erat mūrus domuī utrīque commūnis.** (43:7)
> *There was a wall common to both houses.*

B. Ablative Case

A noun (or pronoun) and a participle in the ablative case form an *ablative absolute*, an adverbial phrase separate from the rest of the sentence and often set off with commas (see page 19). Ablative absolutes are best translated in English with clauses introduced by *when, although, since,* or *if*:

> **Titus . . . , pecūniā datā, in vestibulum ingressus est.** (41:4)
> *Titus . . . , when he had given his money, entered the vestibule.*

Since classical Latin has no present participle for the verb **esse**, ablative absolutes sometimes consist only of two nouns in the ablative case:

> **Titō prīncipe**
> *Titus (being) Emperor*
> *When Titus is (was) Emperor*

II. VERBS

Several impersonal verbal phrases and impersonal verbs were introduced in earlier books. In Book 4 you have met the following new *impersonal verbs*:

> **"Festīnāre tē oportet."** (49:10–11)
> *It is necessary for you to hurry*, better English, *You must hurry.*
> **"Nōn decet patrem,' inquit, 'dēspondēre fīliam. . . .'"** (49:18)

> *"'It is not fitting for a father,' she said, 'to betroth his daughter. . . .'"* better English, *"'A father should not,' she said, 'betroth his daughter. . . .'"*

Some impersonal verbs take an accusative direct object and a genitive expressing cause:

> **"Mē taedet sōlitūdinis."** (49:2–3)
> *It wearies me because of loneliness*, better English, *I am tired of loneliness.*

III. SENTENCES

A. Subordinate Clauses with the Subjunctive

1. If a subordinate clause has its verb in the subjunctive, the tense of the subjunctive is determined by the following rules for the *sequence of tenses* (see page 77):

When the verb in the main clause is in the present or future tense (*primary sequence*), a present subjunctive in the subordinate clause indicates an action going on at the same time as (or subsequent to) that of the main verb, and a perfect subjunctive in the subordinate clause indicates an action that took place before that of the main verb.

When the verb in the main clause is in a past tense (*secondary sequence*), an imperfect subjunctive in the subordinate clause indicates an action going on at the same time as (or subsequent to) that of the main verb, and a pluperfect subjunctive indicates an action that took place before that of the main verb.

Note that sometimes the perfect tense has the force of a present tense (e.g., *I have ordered*) instead of a simple past (*I ordered*). In this case, primary sequence is followed:

> **". . . dominus imperāvit ut iānua claudātur."** (Exercise 50d, No. 10)
> *". . . the master has ordered that the door be closed."*

Here the present instead of the imperfect subjunctive is used after the main verb in the perfect tense, because the perfect tense here clearly implies present time (*the master has ordered*).

2. **Indirect Questions**

When questions are stated indirectly, their verbs are put into the subjunctive, following the sequence of tenses outlined above:

a. **Nōn intellegō cūr servae mē neglegant.**

I *do* not *understand* why the slave girls *neglect* me.

b. **Nōn intellegō cūr servae mē neglēxerint.**
I *do* not *understand* why the slave-girls *neglected* me.

c. **Nōn intellegēbam cūr servae mē neglegerent.**
I *did* not *understand* why the slave-girls *were neglecting* me.

d. **Nōn intellegēbam cūr servae mē neglēxissent.**
I *did* not *understand* why the slave-girls *had neglected* me.

3. Cum Circumstantial Clauses

The conjunction **cum** may introduce a clause that describes the circumstances or the situation prior to or simultaneous with the action of the main clause. When the verb in the main clause is in a past tense (*secondary sequence*), the verb of the **cum** circumstantial clause must be in the subjunctive. It will be an imperfect subjunctive if the clause describes circumstances simultaneous with the action of the verb in the main clause, and it will be a pluperfect subjunctive if the clause describes circumstances prior to the action of the main verb (see pages 9 and 11):

> . . . **cum omnēs dormīrent, ego surrēxī.** . . . (40:32)
> . . . *when all were sleeping, I got up.* . . .
> **Quō cum Titus pervēnisset,** . . . **in vestibulum ingressus est.** (41:4)
> *When Titus had arrived there,* . . . *he entered the entrance hall.*

4. Cum Causal Clauses

Cum may introduce a clause that states a reason or gives a cause. If the verb in the main clause is in the present or future tense (*primary sequence*), the present or perfect subjunctive is used in the causal clause; if the main verb is in a past tense (*secondary sequence*), the imperfect or pluperfect subjunctive is used in the causal clause (see pages 9 and 11):

> **Hīc, cum calōrem et vapōrem vix patī possent, haud multum morābantur.** (41:12–13)
> *Here, since they could scarcely stand the heat and the steam, they did not stay long.*
> **Cum diū ambulāvissent, dēfessī erant.** (Exercise 41c:8)
> *Since they had walked a long time, they were tired.*

5. Result Clauses

The result of an action described in the main clause of a sentence may be expressed by a subordinate clause introduced by **ut** (positive) or **ut nōn** (negative); the present subjunctive is used in primary sequence and the imperfect subjunctive (or sometimes the perfect subjunctive) in secondary sequence. Result clauses are usually anticipated in the main clause by a word such as **adeō** so, **sīc** thus, in this way, **tālis** such, **tam** so, and **tantum** so much, so much:

a. Primary sequence:

> **"Pater tantum temporis in tablīnō agit ut eum numquam videam."** (49:4)
> *"Father spends so much time in the study that I never see him."*

b. Secondary sequence with imperfect subjunctive (see page 78):

> **Cornēlia adeō perturbāta erat ut vix loquī posset.** . . . (49:23)
> *Cornelia was so confused that she was scarcely able to speak.* . . .

c. Secondary sequence with perfect subjunctive (use of this tense puts a special emphasis on the result that took place):

> **Leō tantus et tam ferōx erat ut servus metū exanimātus ceciderit.** (Exercise 49b, No. 2)
> *The lion was so large and so fierce that the slave fell down, paralyzed with fear.*

d. Negative with **ut . . . nōn** (see page 75):

> **Adeō perturbāta est ut loquī nōn possit.** (page 75)
> *She is so confused that she cannot speak.*

6. Telling to, Asking to: Indirect Commands

Direct requests or commands such as **In ātrium prōcēdite!** *Step forward into the atrium!* may be stated indirectly in clauses introduced by **ut** for a positive command or **nē** for a negative command, with the verb in the subjunctive (present in primary sequence and imperfect in secondary sequence). Indirect commands are usually translated with infinitives in English (see page 85):

a. Primary sequence (positive):

> **Cornēlius convīvās omnēs invītat ut in ātrium prōcēdant.** (Exercise 50d, No. 1)

Cornelius invites all the guests to step forward into the atrium.

b. Primary sequence (negative):

Tē semper moneō nē in mediā viā ambulēs. (Exercise 50e, No. 2)
I am always warning you not to walk in the middle of the street.

c. Secondary sequence (positive):

. . . Aurēlia Viniam . . . invītāverat ut prōnuba esset.
(Exercise 49c, lines 4–5)
. . . Aurelia had invited Vinia to be the bride's attendant.

d. Secondary sequence (negative):

Hī iānitōrem ōrābant nē sē dīmitteret. (50:13)
These were begging the doorkeeper not to send them away.

7. Purpose Clauses

The purpose for which the action described in the main clause of a sentence is undertaken may be expressed by a subordinate clause introduced by **ut** (positive) or **nē** (negative); the present subjunctive is used in primary sequence and the imperfect subjunctive in secondary sequence. Purpose clauses are sometimes translated with infinitives in English (see page 100):

a. Primary sequence (positive):

Iānitor baculum habet ut clientēs repellat. (Exercise 52b, No. 2)
The doorkeeper has a stick to drive off clients.

b. Primary sequence (negative):

Cavēte nē cadātis, amīcī!
(Exercise 52b, No. 4)
Watch out that you don't fall, friends!

c. Secondary sequence (positive):

Ancillae hūc illūc concursābant ut omnia parārent. (52:2–3)
The slave-women were running this way and that to get everything ready.

d. Secondary sequence (negative)

. . . nova nūpta super līmen sublāta est nē lāberētur. (52:21–22)
. . . the bride was carried over the threshold so she would not stumble.

B. Indirect Statement

A number of verbs of saying, hoping, thinking, perceiving, and feeling may be followed by the accusative and infinitive construction (indirect statement). The tense of the infinitive in the indirect statement is the same as the tense of the verb in the original, direct statement.

When translating into English, the present infinitive in the indirect statement will be translated with the same tense as that of the verb in the main clause; a future infinitive will be translated to show action subsequent to that of the verb in the main clause; and a perfect infinitive will be translated to show time prior to that of the verb in the main clause:

1. Verb of main clause in *present* tense:

a. **Pater est crūdēlis.**
Putō patrem esse crūdēlem.
(44:4)
I think that father is cruel.
(Present active infinitive replaces present active indicative of the original statement; see page 36. Note the agreement of **patrem** and **crūdēlem**.)

b. **Leōnēs in arēnam immituntur.**
Vidētisne leōnēs in arēnam immittī? (48:10)
Do you see that the lions are being sent into the arena?
(Present passive infinitive replaces present passive indicative of the original statement; see page 55.)

c. **Tū crās nōn labōrābis.**
Prō certō habeō tē crās nōn labōrātūrum esse. (45:5)
I am certain that you will not work tomorrow.
(Future active infinitive replaces future active indicative of the original statement; see page 43.)

d. **Hoc per iocum dīxī.**
Nōnne sentīs mē per iocum hoc dīxisse? (45:11)
Surely you realize that I said this as a joke, don't you?
(Perfect active infinitive replaces perfect active indicative of the original statement; see page 43.)

e. **Servus ā prīncipe arcessītus est.**
Videō servum ā prīncipe arcessītum esse. (48:20)
I see that the slave was summoned by the emperor.
(Perfect passive infinitive replaces perfect passive indicative of the original statement; see page 55.)

2. Verb of main clause in *past* tense:

a. **Titus sē discēdere nōn vult.**
Respondit Titum sē discēdere nōlle. (46:27)

He replied that Titus <u>did not want</u> to leave.

(Present active infinitive replaces present active indicative of the original statement; see page 51.)

b. **Prīnceps ā gladiātōribus <u>salūtātur</u>.**
Vīdī prīncipem ā gladiātōribus <u>salūtārī</u>. (Exercise 46c, lines 8–9).
I saw the emperor <u>being greeted</u> by the gladiators.

(Present passive infinitive replaces present passive indicative of the original statement; see page 55.)

c. **Merīdiānī mox in arēnam <u>venient</u>.**
Respondit Titus merīdiānōs mox in arēnam <u>ventūrōs esse</u>. (46:27–28)
Titus replied that the midday fighters <u>would</u> soon <u>come</u> into the arena.

(Future active infinitive replaces future active indicative of the original statement; see page 51.)

d. **Titus iam <u>cōnsēdit</u>.**
Subitō vīdit Titum iam <u>cōnsēdisse</u>. (46:7–8)
Suddenly he saw that Titus <u>had</u> already <u>taken his seat</u>.

(Perfect active infinitive replaces perfect active indicative of the direct statement; see page 51.)

e. **Titus eō iam <u>ductus est</u>.**
Vīdimus Titum eō iam <u>ductum esse</u>. (Exercise 46c, line 7)
We saw that Titus <u>had</u> already <u>been led</u> to that place.

(Perfect passive infinitive replaces perfect passive indicative of the original statement; see page 55.)

3. A reflexive pronoun or adjective in an indirect statement refers to the subject of the verb in the main clause that introduces the indirect statement (see pages 43–44):

Mārcus dīcit <u>sē</u> in lūdum ventūrum esse.
Marcus that <u>he</u> will go to school.
Puellae puerīs dīxērunt <u>sē</u> eōs adiūtūrās esse. (page 44)
The girls told the boys that <u>they</u> would help them.
Puerī dīxērunt puellās <u>sē</u> adiūtūrās esse.
The boys said that the girls would help <u>them</u>.